AUTHOR'S NOTES

As much has been written about this Rebellion, it is unnecessary for me to give the history of that time, except for a summary of events.

Natal Militia Order No. 128, sets out the conditions of the award - conditions, that seemed to have been stretched a bit, for, medals without clasps, were awarded to certain Chiefs who remained loyal to the Natal Government; perhaps, however, their remaining loyal, could be construed as having rendered "valuable service".

The Goldsmiths and Silversmiths Ltd., of London (now Garrard & Co. Ltd.), designed, manufactured and apparently also named the medals. The naming, on Officers medals, was hand engraved in an attractive script, whilst medals to Warrant Officers, Non-Commissioned Officers, and men, were impressed rather lightly, in squarish capitals. Elected Chief Leaders and Sub-Leaders of the Militia Reserves, who were in fact of Officer rank, however, had the naming of their medals in the same form as did the Warrant Officers, Non-Commissioned Officers and men.

The medal was of a good quality silver to all ranks, but Bronze trial strikings do exist - apparently from the same date as the silver medal.

DESCRIPTION OF THE MEDAL

Obverse: The coinage head of King Edward VII facing right, with legend:

"EDWARDVS VII REX IMPERATOR"

Reverse: In the centre are figures of BRITTANNIA and NATALIA. The former is holding an orb, surmounted by the figure of Peace in her left hand, and Natalia is holding a large sword in her right hand. In the background are some natives and a kraal.
In the exergue is the word NATAL.

Size: 1.42 inches - 36.2mm

Ribbon: 1.25 inches - 31.76mm wide   Crimson with black edges

Suspension: By a plain, straight suspender

Clasps: One - 1906

(The above description is from BRITISH BATTLES & MEDALS by Major L.L. Gordon - 4th Edition)

* * * * *

The total of medals listed in this work is 9979, and of these 1934 were without the clasp 1906. A full summary of these figures is shown later on in this work.

* * * * *

In his book "RELUCTANT REBELLION - The 1906 - 1908 DISTURBANCES IN NATAL" S. Marks says, on page 244:-

"When in September McCallum requested that Imperial war medals be struck for the men "who distinguished themselves in the recent battle", the great disparity in the numbers killed and the whole nature of the campaign led Churchill to minute, in typically uninhibited fashion:-

> "There was, I think, nearly a dozen casualties among these devoted men in the course of their prolonged operations and more than even four or five are dead on the field of honour. In these circumstances it is evident that special consideration should be shown to the survivors. But I should hesitate to press upon them an Imperial Medal, in view of the distaste which this Colony has so strongly evinced for outside interference of all kinds. A Copper medal bearing BAMBATH'S head, to be struck at the expense of the Colony, seems to be the most appropriate memento of their sacrifice and their triumphs."

Marks, on page XVI, estimates that between 3500 and 4000 Africans lost their lives during the disturbances (this refers, of course, to those Africans who sided with the enemy.) Some two dozen whites, including about half a dozen civilians, were also killed; although no white women or children were harmed in any way, and white property remained relatively unscathed.
On page 214 of the same book the Indian Stretcher Bearers Corps is mentioned viz:-

"From Johannesburg, too, MOHANDAS K. GANDHI, imbued with the belief that:-
    "The British Empire existed for the world (and) --- a genuine sense of loyalty, wrote to the Governor of Natal offering Indian aid. After some hesitation, the Government invited them to accompany the white troops as an ambulance Corps. Twenty-five stretcher-bearers, under Sergeant - Major M.K. Ghandhi, were provided and paid for by the Natal Indian Congress."
M.K. Gandhi was later to become the Prime Minister of India - he was assassinated on 31.1.1948.

Eric Goetche in his "Natal Mounted Rifles History" on page 111 tells of Lt.Blamey's gallantry, which was lauded by all those present. Many thought his action worthy of a Victoria Cross. Major (Doctor) S.G. Campbell, Durban Light Infantry, under whose command Blamey fell, was so greatly impressed by his outstanding act of valour, that, after due deliberation, he strongly recommended that Blamey be awarded a decoration.

Major Dymock (Dimmick) of the Natal Police considered it an outstanding act of valour, on the part of Blamey, and he, with other Officers sent in a report to the General Officer Commanding General Dartnell, recommending that Blamey be awarded the Victoria Cross. This recommendation was placed before the Govenor of Natal, Col.Sir Henry McCallum KCMG, who immediately forwarded it overseas. Sir Henry promised to see H.M. the King personally on this matter.

In due course Lt. Blamey received but a MENTION for Distinguished Conduct in the field.

The act of valour in which Lt. Blamey figured so bravely was the rescue of Cpl. Richard (Dick) L. Acutt, (and not Cpl. Arnott as per Militia orders in the Natal Government Gazette of 26.6.1903) under trying conditions, in the action at Nkomo Hill area. Fuller details are given in later pages. Captain R. Armstrong of the NMR, who is also mentioned later on, however, received no recognition whatsoever.

* * * * *

KILLED IN ACTION

Corporal	ALEXANDER E.	Roystons Horse	3rd June 1906
Trooper	ARMSTRONG G.	Natal Police	8th February 1906
Trooper	ASHTON A.H.	Natal Police	4th April 1906
Trooper	BOUCK J.L.	Roystons Horse	3rd June 1906
2c.Serjeant	BROWN E.T.N.	Natal Police	4th April 1906
L/Corporal	CHRISTOPHER V.J.M.	Natal Carbineers	5th July 1906
Trooper	GREENWOOD J.P.	Natal Police	4th April 1906
Trooper	HARDING J.	Roystons Horse	3rd June 1906
L/Serjeant	HARRISON J.C.G.	Natal Police	4th April 1906
Sub.Insp.	HUNT S.H.K.	Natal Police	8th February 1906
Trooper	KNIGHT R.B.	Tvl. Mtd. Rifles	2nd July 1906
Captain	McFARLANE S.C. (DSO)	Tvl. Mtd. Rifles	10th June 1906
Trooper	POWELL A.	Natal Mtd. Rifles	19th June 1906
Trooper	ROBERTSON S.I.	Roystons Horse	3rd June 1906
Trooper	STEEL H.S.	Umvoti Division Res.	28th May 1906

DIED ON SERVICE

Trooper	BULL W.G.	Natal Mtd. Rifles	15th May 1906
Trooper	CLEMENTS S.T.	Natal Mtd. Rifles	28th June 1906
Trooper	CRISP A.J.	Natal Mtd. Rifles	Not Known
Private	McINNES A.	Natal Rangers	8th July 1906
Private	OHLSON C.	2nd Roystons Horse	29th July 1906
Trooper	STRECKER F.C.	Roystons Horse	10th May 1906
Trooper	WALSH M.G.	Roystons Horse	3rd May 1906

DIED OF WOUNDS

Trooper	COLL C.	Zululand Mtd. Rifles	
Trooper	GLOVER F.H.	Tvl. Mtd. Rifles	13th June 1906
Trooper	HAWKINS J.	Roystons Horse	3rd June 1906
Trooper	MAW H.C.	Tvl. Mtd. Rifles	14th May 1906
Trooper	STEYN H.W.	Tvl. Mtd. Rifles	20th June 1906

* * * * *

HONOURS & AWARDS

OFFICERS

Knight Commander The Most Distinguished Order of St. Michael and St. George KCMG

Col. Duncan McKENZIE CB CMG VD
      Natal Carbineers

* * *

Promoted to Hon. Lieut.Colonel in the Army

Lt.Col. J.R. ROYSTON CMG DSO
         Roystons Horse

* * *

Distinguished Service Order DSO

Col. H.T. BRU-de-WOLD CMG VD
      Natal Militia Staff

Col. G. LEUCHARS CMG
      Umvoti Mounted Rifles

* * *

Mentioned for Distinguished Conduct in the Field

Capt. E.G. CLERK   Roystons Horse
       Natal Gazette - 26th June 1906

Lieut. A.H.G. BLAMEY   Natal Mtd. Rifles
       Natal Gazette - 26th June 1906

Insp. O. DIMMICK   Natal Police
       Natal Gazette - 3rd July 1906
       (Roll shows Major. O. Dimmick)

Tpr.   C.W. GUEST   Natal Police
       Natal Gazette - 26th June 1906

Tpr.   W.C. HOLMES   Roystons Horse
       Natal Gazette - 26th June 1906

* * *

Mentioned for Meritorious Service

Col.	Sir A. WOOLLS SAMPSON KCB		Major	W. MURRAY-SMITH Natal Mounted Rifles
Lt.Col.	J. HYSLOP DSO VD Natal Militia Staff		Major	W.A. VAN DER PLANK Zululand Mounted Rifles
Lt.Col.	T. McCUBBIN CMG Commandant Durban		Major	S.B. WOLLATT Natal Veterinary Corps
Lt.Col.	M.C. ROWLAND Staff Officer Transvaal		Capt.	C.V. HOSKEN Transport Natal Militia Staff
Lt.Col.	J.S. WYLIE Durban Light Infantry		Capt.	G.A. LABISTOUR Natal Royal Regiment
Major	R.A. BUNTINE Natal Medical Corps		Capt.	M.G. PEARSON Natal Medical Corps
Major	S.G. CAMPBELL Durban Light Infantry		Capt.	A. PRIOR Natal Service Corps
Major	S. CARTER Umvoti Mounted Rifles		Lt.	J.S. HEDGES Zululand Mounted Rifles
Major	W.H. SMITH Natal Mounted Rifles		Chief Leader	J.A. NEL Umvoti Mounted Reserves

* * *

WARRANT OFFICERS, NON-COMMISSIONED OFFICERS & MEN

Distinguished Conduct Medal DCM
Natal Gazette - 10th September 1907

Sqd. Sjt.Maj.	W. CALVERLEY Zululand Mounted Rifles		Sjt.	S. TITLESTAD Zulu Mounted Rifles
Sjt.	C.W. GUEST Natal Police		Farr. Sjt.	C.B. MITCHELL Transvaal Mounted Rifles
Tpr.	O.L.M. FOLKER Natal Police		Tpr.	W. DEELEY Zululand Mounted Rifles
Tpr.	W. JOHNSON Zululand Mounted Rifles	-	Roll shows Folker as 2c Sjt.	
Tpr.	G.W. OLIVIER Zululand Mounted Rifles	-	Roll shows him as C.W. Johnson	
		-	Roll shows him as G.O. Olivier	

* * *

Meritorious Service Medal   MSM
Natal Gazette - 10th September 1907

RSM	J. WEBBER Roystons Horse		Sjt.	G.P. BAGNALL Natal Medical Corps
	J.A. BUTCHER Natal Service Corps		Sjt.	E.B. BRAND Transvaal Mounted Rifles
	T.P. CATCHPOLE Natal Carbineers	-	Roll shows him as S/Sjt. I.A. Butcher	
	J.F. CRAWFORD Natal Telegraph Corps	-	Roll shows him as Tpr. T.P. Catchpole	
	E.I. DICKS Natal Carbineers	-	Roll shows him as Cpl. J.F. Crawford	

H.G. Le MESURIER Natal Mounted Rifles	–	Roll shows him as Tpr. H.E. Le Mesurier	
F.L. MALAN Transvaal Mounted Rifles			
J.F. PEMBERTON Natal Telegraph Corps	–	Roll shows him as Tpr. J.P. Pemberton	
I.E. SJOBLOM Natal Mounted Rifles	–	Roll shows him as Tpr. I.E. Sjoblom	
S.J. WADMAN Natal Mounted Rifles	–	Roll shows him as Sjt. A.J. Wadman	

* * *

Good Service

The Natal Gazette of 10th September 1907, lists the names of 85 men for good service.

* * *

DUPLICATE ISSUES

The following had Duplicate Medals issued and where possible the reason for the issue of a duplicate is listed:-

Rank	Name	Unit	Reason
Pte/Tpr.	ACKERMAN J.	Melmoth Reserves/ Zululand Mounted Rifles	On two Rolls
Pte/Tpr.	ADENDORFF H.J.C.	Natal Royal Regt./ Umvoti Mounted Rifles	On two Rolls
Seaman Tpr.	AGNEW J. AGNEW J.	Natal Naval Corps Roystons Horse	On two Rolls The same man
Pte.	BESWICK F.	Roystons Horse Durban Militia Reserves	On two Rolls
Tpr/Pte.	BINDON W.E.	Roystons Horse & Natal Royal Regt.	On two Rolls
Tpr.	BLAKE R.H.	Natal Telegraphic Corps & Supplementary Roll	On two Rolls
Tpr. Seaman	BUCHANAN D. BUCHANAN D.	Roystons Horse & Natal Naval Corps	On two Rolls The same man
SSM	CALVERLEY W.J.	Zululand Mtd. Rifles & Supplementary List.	On two Rolls
Pte/Tpr.	CAMERON J.	Natal Royal Regiment & Roystons Horse	On two Rolls
Tpr.	CARTER R.W.	Natal Mounted Rifles & Roystons Horse	On two Rolls
Tpr.	CASTLE F.	Roystons Horse	Had a 2nd re-engraved. Medal issued to replace original lost. Nov. 1957.
Tpr.	CHAMBERS R.R.	Natal Police Roystons Horse	On two Rolls
Pte.	CLARKE J.L.	Natal Rangers	Had a 2nd re-engraved. Medal issued 1950 to replace original lost one.
Tpr.	COLE J.	Natal Mounted Rifles & Roystons Horse	On two Rolls

Cpl.	COUZENS J.C.	Natal Royal Regiment & Roystons Horse	On two Rolls
Pte.	DAY A.F.	Melmoth Reserves &	The same man
Tpr.	DAY A.T.	Zululand Mounted Rifles	on two Rolls
Tpr.	DEAN H.	Transvaal Mounted Rifles	Re-engraved medal issued August 1957.
Tpr.	EDWARDS D.R.	Natal Mounted Rifles & Roystons Horse	On two Rolls
Pte/Tpr.	FAY J.	Lancs & Yorks Contg & Roystons Horse	On two Rolls
Tpr.	FRAME D.	Natal Police	To replace a lost medal. 2nd medal not re-engraved. Issued from blank stock.
Pte/Tpr.	FERREIRA S.P.	Melmoth Reserves & Zululand Mounted Rifles	On two Rolls
Tpr.	GELL E.H.T.	Natal Mounted Rifles	A duplicate issued 6th September 1912.
Wdr.	GORDON A.	Natal Police	Name twice on same Roll
Tpr.	GROVE R.B.W.	Natal Police	To replace a lost medal.
Pte/Tpr.	HENNESSEY E.J.A.	Natal Royal Regiment Roystons Horse	On two Rolls
Pte/Tpr.	HILL F.	Natal Royal Regiment Roystons Horse	On two Rolls
Pte.	HODNETT B.G.	Natal Royal Regiment	The same man
Tpr.	HODNETT H.	Roystons Horse	on two Rolls
Pte/Tpr.	HUMPHREY F.	Natal Royal Regiment & Roystons Horse	On two Rolls
Tpr.	INGRAM J.H.	Roystons Horse	A 2nd medal issued (re-engraved)
Pte.	JONES J.	Natal Rangers	A 2nd medal issued (re-engraved)
Pte.	KELLY M.	Newcastle Division Res.	A 2nd medal issued 10th June 1912 (re-engraved)
Pte.	KEYS R.G.	Lancs & Yorks Contg.	A 2nd(re-engraved) medal issued Feb.1913.
Sjt/Tpr.	KRUGER E.H.C.	Melnoth Reserves/ Zulandland Mounted Rifles	On two Rolls
Pte/Tpr.	LANG A.	Natal Royal Regiment & Umvoti Mounted Regt.	On two Rolls
Pte/Tpr.	LILLE J.	Natal Royal Regiment & Roystons Horse	On two Rolls
Pte/Tpr.	LOXLEY H.	Natal Royal Regiment & Roystons Horse	On two Rolls
Bmbr.	MAJOR H.	Natal Field Artillery "B" Battery	A 2nd medal (re-engraved) Issued February 1913.
Pte.	MARTIN H.	Durban Light Infantry	To replace a medal lost. (Re-engraced 10th June 1912)

Col.	MITCHELL J.C.	No unit given	A duplicate issued for a collection.
Tpr.	NEILSON N.V.	Natal Police	A 2nd (re-engraved) medal issued.
Pte/Tpr.	NEL G.	Natal Royal Regiment & Roystons Horse	On two Rolls
Tpr.	NOLAN J.	Roystons Horse	Deceased. The duplicate issued from blank stock.
Pte/Tpr.	POLLARD J.	Natal Royal Regiment & Roystons Horse	On two Rolls
Leader/Tpr.	PRETORIUS A.L.	Melmoth Reserves/ Zululand Mounted Rifles	On two Rolls
Tpr.	ROCHE H.	Natal Police/ Roystons Horse	On two Rolls
Tpr.	ROY J.	Roystons Horse	A 2nd (re-engraved) medal in 1939.
Tpr.	RUDLAND L.	Natal Carbineers/ Roystons Horse	On two Rolls
Pte.	SALTER S.B.	Durban Militia Reserve	The same man on two Rolls.
Tpr.	SALTER S.	Roystons Horse	
Sjt.	SCHALLENBERG H.W.F.	New Hanover Reserves	The same man on two Rolls.
Tpr.	SCHALLENBERG H.W.F.	Umvoti Mounted Rifles	
Seam	SHAND G.T.	Natal Naval Corps	Duplicate issued 1912. Original lost.
Pte.	SHEFFIELD A.	Natal Medical Corps Roystons Horse	On two Rolls
Tpr.	URQUHART J.	Natal Mounted Rifles & Roystons Horse	On two Rolls
Pte/Tpr.	VAN BLERCK A.	Natal Royal Regiment & Roystons Horse	On two Rolls
Pte/Tpr.	VAN RENSBERG M.L.	Natal Royal Regiment & Roystons Horse	On two Rolls
Pte/Tpr.	VENTER N.	Natal Royal Regiment & Roystons Horse	On two Rolls
Tpr.	WALLER T.	2nd Roystons Horse	A 2nd (re-engraved) medal issued. July 1960.
Pte.	WARWICK C.C.	Natal Medical Corps & Umvoti Division Res.	On two Rolls
Tpr.	WILLET H.G.	Natal Police	A 2nd (re-engraved) medal issued Sept. 1912.
Sjt.	WILLIS J.M.	Durban Light Infantry	Twice on same Roll
Pte/Tpr.	WINTERBOER W.	Natal Royal Regt./ Roystons Horse	On two Rolls
Pte.	WRIGHT E.J.	Natal Rangers	A 2nd (re-engraved) medal issued.
Tpr.	ZONDO GOGOLOLO	Natal Native Horse	Twice on same Roll

Notes:
1. No indication has been found as to the method of renaming these medals.

2. A re-rngraved medal for Tpr. F. Castle was delivered to Franz Graf Schlick, of Schloss Lebenberg, Kitzbuhel, Tirol, Austria, on 1.11.1957. The name "CASTLE" had been used by Schlick as a pseudonym. His original medal was confiscated by American Occupation troops in 1945.

3. It is not claimed that this is a complete list of duplicates, for no accurate records, in this regard, were maintained.

MEDALS OFFICIALLY RE-ENGRAVED & RE-ISSUED

Pte.	ALLEY W.T.	Natal Rangers. Re-issued 8th May 1950 to Pte. J.L. Clarke. Natal Rangers.
Pte.	APPALSAMY	Indian Stretcher Bearer Corps. Re-engraved March 1962.
Pack Leader	AYASAMI	Natal Civilian Employee
Pte.	BARTLEY A.	Natal Rangers - Re-issued to Tpr. T. Walker. 2nd Roystons Horse.
No Rank	BAYEKANA	Intelligence. Re-issued Chief Mveli.
Pack Leader	BEGIZULU	Natal Civilian Employee. Re-issued Sept. 1912 to Tpr. H.G. Willet Natal Police
Pte.	BLACKADDER A.	Cape Mounted Rifleman. Re-issued August 1957 to Tpr. H. Dean Tvl. Mounted Rifles.
Tpr.	BUCK T.J.	Zululand Mounted Rifles. Re-engraved 9th April 1962.
Tpr.	CAMERON D.A.	Natal Telegraphic Corps
Tpr.	COOKE B.	Roystons Horse. Re-engraved Nov. 1957 for Tpr. F. Casyle Roystons Horse.
RSM	DODD G.F.	New Hanover Reserves.
Tpr.	DUNN R.	Intelligence Service
Tpr.	EVANS W.G.	Roystons Horse
Tpr.	FOLEY J.	Roystons Horse
Pack Leader	FRED	Natal Civilian Employee. Re-engraved for Pte. H. Martin Durban Light Infantry.
No Rank	GEORGE	Intelligence - Re-engraved for Chief Nyonigeywa
Tpr.	GRIEVE D.	Natal Native Horse
Pack Leader	JAN	Natal Civilian Employee. Re-engraved February 1913 for Bmdr. H. Major Natal Field Arty. "B" Battery"
Pte.	JENKINS J.	Natal Rangers
Pack Leader	JOHANN	Natal Civilian Employee
Pte.	JONES J.	Natal Rangers - Re-engraved 1939 for Tpr. J. Roy Roystons Horse
Seaman	JOHNSTONE W.H.	Natal Naval Corps
Pte.	KAHN M.	Indian Stretcher Bearer Corps

Tpr.	KELVIE J.	Roystons Horse
Tpr.	KILGOUR P.	Natal Carbineers
Gnr.	KILMISTER M.H.	Natal Field Artillery "Pom Pom" Section
Pte.	KILPATRICK W.	Durban Light Infantry
Sjt.	KUNZ J.J.	Umvoti Division Reserves
Pack Leader	Kuppan	Natal Civilian Employee. Re-engraved for R.G. Keys February 1913.
Pte.	LANG A.	Natal Royal Regiment
Tpr.	LAWSON R.	Natal Carbineers
Tpr.	LEVETT P.A.	Roystons Horse
Pte.	LLOYD W.H.	Durban Light Infantry
Pack Leader	MAHOMMED	Natal Civilian Employee. Re-engraved 10th June 1912 for Pte. M. Kelly Newcastle Division Reserves
Tpr.	MAKABELA HARRY	Natal Native Horse. Re-engraved 15th June 1917 for Pte. E.J. Wright Natal Rangers
Tpr.	McMAHON M.	Roystons Horse
Tpr.	MURPHY C.	Roystons Horse
Leader	NIENABER B.J.	Kilp River Reserves
Pack Leader	NKOSANA	Natal Civilian Employee. Re-engraved to Seaman G.T. Shand. Natal Naval Corps.
Capt.	O'NEILL O.A.	Natal Veterinary Corps
Tpr.	PEMBERTHY J.	Transvaal Mounted Rifles
Tpr.	PERRY S.S.J.	Roystons Horse
Pte.	PETERS L.	Durban Light Infantry
Tpr.	PIETERSE M.J.C.	Northern Dist. Mounted Rifles
Tpr.	POTGIETER A.M.	Natal Police
Tpr.	REID T.H.	Natal Carbineers
Tpr.	REISE G.A.	Natal Police
Cpl.	SILAMELA JOHN	Natal Native Horse. Re-engraved 15th March 1962
Pte.	TAIT J.	Melmoth Reserves
Pack Leader	TOGWAYO	Natal Civilian Employee. Re-engraved for Tpr. J.H. Ingram. Roystons Horse.
Gaoler	TURNER F.E.	Natal Police
Tpr.	VAN ROOYEN G.H.	Krantzkop Reserves
Tpr.	VAN ROOYEN T.J.J.	Umvoti Mounted Rifles
Tpr.	VAN VUREN W.F.	Natal Police
Sub-Leader	VERMAAK C.J.	Umvoti Division Reserves
Tpr.	VINOE J.	Roystons Horse

Rank	Name	Unit
Pte.	WATSON W.	Natal Rangers
Pte.	WATSON W.A.	Durban Militia Reserves
Cpl.	YOUNG W.	Lancs. & Yorks Contingent
No Rank	ZINKE	Intelligence - Re-engraved for Chief Sibindi.
Tpr.	ZONDO G.	Natal Native Horse

* * *

Note:
No accurate records in this regard were kept - there could, therefore, have been further re-engraved medals.

* * *

MEDALS AWARDED BUT WITHDRAWN OR WITHHELD FOR VARIOUS REASONS

Pte.	BAILEY J.G. Natal Royal Regiment	Tpr.	JOHNSON W. Natal Mounted Rifles
Tpr.	BECKLEY P.G. Natal Police	Tpr.	KUBHEKA MTSHUMAYELI Natal Native Horse
Pte.	BORLAND A.S. Natal Royal Regiment	Tpr.	LEE R.J. Natal Police
Tpr.	BURNE A.F. Natal Police	Tpr.	LUKE E.P. Natal Mounted Rifles
Tpr.	CASSIDY D. Natal Mounted Rifles	Wdr.	MARVELL A. Natal Police
Pte.	DALEY J. Natal Royal Regiment	Pte.	McGREGOR D. Natal Royal Regiment
Pte.	DONKIN F.W. Natal Royal Regiment	Tpr.	McIVER W.R. Natal Police
Tpr.	FORTMAN J.W. New Hanover Reserves	Tpr.	MICHELSON O. Natal Police
Tpr.	GIBB A.M. Natal Mounted Rifles	Tpr.	MURPHY J. Natal Mounted Rifles
Tpr.	GIBB W. Natal Mounted Rifles	Cons.	MURPHY T. Natal Police
Tpr.	GILLISPIE J. Natal Service Corps	Det.	NEILSON C.W.J. Natal Police
Tpr.	HAWKEN M. Natal Police	Tpr.	OLDFIELD T.S. Natal Police
Cons.	HAYES G.E. Natal Police	Pte.	POLLARD J. Natal Royal Regiment
Tpr.	HINDE A.H. Natal Mounted Rifles	Tpr.	RANS T. Natal Mounted Rifles
Cons.	HOOPER F. Natal Police	Pte.	REARDON P.J.C. Natal Royal Regiment
Tpr.	HORNE P.C. Natal Mounted Rifles	Pte.	RICHARDS J.G. Natal Royal Regiment
Cons.	JOHNSON A. Natal Police	Pte.	RIGBY S. Natal Royal Regiment

Tpr.	SCHONBERG A.C. Natal Police		Tpr.	URQUHART J. Natal Mounted Rifles
Pte.	SIBTHORP A.E. Natal Royal Regiment		Pte.	VON BERG A. Natal Royal Regiment
Con.	SLINEY T. Natal Police		Pte.	VON BERG B. Natal Royal Regiment
Wdr.	TAYLOR H.W. Natal Police		Cons.	YOUNG R. Natal Police
Tpr.	TYMMS A. Natal Mounted Rifles			

* * *

A DIARY OF DAY-TO-DAY OPERATIONS IN THE FIELD

AS TOLD IN OFFICIAL DESPATCHES

A special supplement of the Government Gazette published on October 4th 1906, contained interesting official correspondence, in which is given, a full and consecutive account of the events connected with the rebellion. In order to make the correspodence, and the various matters more easily understood, the following chronology of the campaign is published:-

Feb. 8 — Natives attack mounted police force near Byrnetown; Sub-Inspector Hunt and Trooper Armstrong killed.

Feb. 9 — Martial law proclaimed. Carbineers and Artillery mobilised.

Feb. 10 — Troops depart for Richmond District.

Feb. 11 — Press censorship established. NRR leave for Richomnd.

Feb. 14 — Cameron Highlanders arrive in Maritzburg.

Feb. 15 — Two prisoners shot at Richmond, after court martial trial.

Feb. 20 — Umbeli's men attacked by rebels. Three of the latter killed and several wounded.

Feb. 21 — Alexandra Magistrate, whilst collecting poll tax, is defied by 1,000 natives, and also threaten their own chief.

Feb. 22 — Scare at Greytown; women and children go into laager.

Feb. 23 — Mobilisation of UMR and NMR, - two sections Durban Artillery, two companies Durban Light Infantry, and a half company of Natal Naval Corps.

Feb. 27 — Chief Gobizembi, of Mapumulo, ordered to produce followers who defied Magistrate at Allans.

March 2 — Col. Leuchars sends ultimatum to Gobizembi, who failed to carry out orders.

March 5 — Ultimatum expires; Gobizembi's kraal bombarded. The Chief taken prisoner.

March 7 — Large numbers of surrenders at Mapumulo.

March 16 — NRR return to City.

March 23 — Bambata reported to have been deposed and Funizwe appointed successor, Magwababa made regent.

BRYNETOWN SENTENCES

March 28 — Death sentence upon twelve natives who took part in attack upon the police at Brynetown confirmed by His Excellency the Governor.

March 29		Secretary of State for the Colonies orders the suspension of the sentences pending the receipt of full particulars from His Excellency the Governor. As a protest against the interference of the Imperial Government, the Hon. C.J. Smythe and his colleagues in the Natal Ministry resign.
March 30		Public indignation meetings held in Maritzburg and Durban to protest against Home Government's action. Imperial veto withdrawn. Natal given freedom of action regarding execution. Ministry withdraw their resignation.
March 31		Return of Carbinners and Artillery.
April 2		Execution of condemed natives at Richmond.
April 3		Report of Magwababa's abduction by Bambata received. Small force of police, which was despatched from Greytown to arrest the desposed chief, fired upon by rebels. Force of Police under Col. Mansel despatched to Greytown.
April 4		Escort of police, under Col. Mansel, conveying women and children's from Keat's Drift to Greytown, attacked on Impanz Road. European Casualties, 4 killed and 4 wounded.
April 5		UMR, DLI, and Artillery, under Col. Leuchars, despatched to Greytown.
April 7		Bambata's kraal shelled. Rebels escape to Zululand.
April 17		Left Wing Carbineers mobilised. Dinizulu asserts his loyalty.
April 19		Col. Royston commissioned to raise a corps. Detachment of NRR leave for Greytown.
April 20		Cape Colony offers 500 picked men.
April 23		Transvaal offers 500 men.
April 26		First contingent of Transvaal Mounted Rifles leave Johannesburg for the front. Col. McKay with Left Wing Natal Carbineers arrive at Nkandhla. Right Wing leave for the front.
April 27		Sigananda revolts.
April 30		Royston's Horse depart for the front.
May 1		Cape Government offers Maxim Battery.
May 2		Skirmish at Nkandhla. Four or five natives killed.
May 3		Mr. H.M. Stainbank, Magistrate at Nkandhla, and Trooper Fellers, NP, shot by natives. Mr. Stainbank succumbs.

ATTACK ON MANSEL

May 5		Col. Mansel's force, comprising NP, DLI, NNC, NMR, and Nonqai attacked near Cetewayo's grave by about 200 natives. Latter repulsed with a loss of 60 killed and many wounded. European casualties, one man wounded.
May 8		War Loan Bill (£500,000) passed by Assembly.
May 9		Chief Kula and six indunas arrested.
May 10		Natal Colonist in England offer Rexer guns. Offer accepted.
May 12		Force of 400 men under Major Murray-Smith attack impi near Mteli's kraal. Twenty nine natives killed and many wounded. Col. McKenzie has brush with enemy in Insuzi Valley, killing two.
May 12		Services of 500 Legion of Frontiersmen offered.
May 14		Natal Native Horse leave for the front. Recruiting for Natal Rangers commenced.
May 14		Brush with rebels in Ikombi Valley. Four natives killed. Two rebels killed near Ngosi Hill.

May	16	Mr. Walters, sub-overseer of road party, murdered by natives at Mbizu Stream, Nkandhla.
May	22	Transvaal contingent of Natal Rangers leave Dundee for the Front.
May	24	Natal Rangers (local contingent) leave for the front.
May	27	Three squadrons UMR and one squadron Reserves under Col. Leuchars surprise party of rebels, killing eight. Camp (at Pukinyoni) attacked in evening by force of about 600 strong. Seventy rebels killed. One European killed and three wounded. Two native levies killed and 11 wounded.
May	29	Col. McKenzie's force engage natives near the Insuzi. Forty rebels and one European killed. Government accept Mr. Abe Bailey's offer of 150 volunteers.
May	31	Col. McKenzie's forces meet with enemy and kill 21.
June	1	Sigananda's induna Mpikwa and 76 men surrender. Col. McKenzie's force shells Mome stronghold. Three rebels killed and 24 taken prisoners.
June	3	Troops under Col. McKenzie attacked in Nkandhla Bush. Enemy repulsed with over 140 killed. Five men of Royston's Horse killed and ten wounded.

MOME VALLEY

June	4	Operation in bush. Two natives killed.
June	6	Ten rebels killed in Nkandhla bush.
June	7	Twenty rebels killed. Government accepts Cape offer of Maxim detachment.
June	10	Mome Valley fight. Native losses 350, including Chief Mehlokazulu. Bambata wounded. European casualties, one killed, 9 wounded, one subsequently died.
June	12	Bambata reported dead.
June	13	Sigananda and his son surrender.
June	15	Bambata's death confirmed. Chief Mteli also reported dead.
June	18	Dinizulu's indunas arrived in Maritzburg. 275 rebels aurrendered at Nkandhla. Three stores at Thring's Post attacked by rebels; the storeman and a trooper killed, and one other wounded. Convoy of wagons attacked near Otimati River; one man wounded.
June	19	Col. McKenzie's force meets enemy at Otimati, killing 90 of them.
June	20	Contingent of Durban Reserve despatched to Stanger.
June	21	Further Reserves despatched from Durban.
June	24	Fifty rebels surrendered to Col. McKay. Total number of rebels taken in Nkandhla district to date 806. Col. Royston's Horse perform a sweeping movement. Five rebels killed and 25 taken prisoners.
June	25	Royston continues operation. Nine natives killed and 81 taken prisoners.
June	27	Col. Leuchars comes into contact with the enemy near Messini's location, who are repulsed with a loss of 60 killed and many wounded.
June	28	Sigananda sentenced to death.
June	29	Col. Royston's column operates through Qudeni bush. Three rebels killed and 25 captured.

CONVOY ATTACKED

July	1	Mr. Oliver Veal murdered at Messini's kraal.
July	2	Transport convoy of 140 men attacked between Bond's Drift and Thring's Post by 500 natives. Rebels repulsed with a loss of 40 killed. One trooper

		ZMR killed and one missing. Impi 1,500 strong attack Col. Barker's advance guard in Noodsberg district close to the Insuzi, advancing to within five yards of troops. Repulsed with loss of 600 killed. One European killed and two wounded.
July	3	Various columns endeavour to close in upon Messini's main impi. Number of rebels killed by total forces 400.
July	4	Col. McKenzie makes another drive, nineteen natives killed.
July	7	Combined forces engage in a bush drive, six rebels killed. Bishop of Zululand charges members of Royston's Horse with shooting prisoners in cold blood.
July	8	Three columns under Col. McKenzie surround Matshwili's impi near Insimbi Stream in the Mba Valley. No fewer than 547 rebels killed.
July	14	Court of enquiry find allegations of Bishop pf Zululand not proved and hold that prisoners were shot according to military law in attempting to escape.
July	16	Sections of Home Press incensed at report of decapitation of Bambata and alleged massacre by friendlies at Mome.
July	17	Allegations of massacre refuted in Natal Legislative Assembly.
July	18	Debate in House of Commons regarding allegations.
July	22	Total number of surrenders during eight days armistice 1,047.
July	23	NRR return to Maritzburg and disband. Sigananda dies from matural causes.
July	26	TMR return to the Rand.
July	29	TMR and DLI arrive in Durban. Bishop of Zululand demans civil enquiry into allegations against Royston's Horse.
July	30	Royston's Horse arrive in Maritzburg. Mid-Illovo Chief Tilonka court-martialled on charge of sedition.
July	31	Troops at the front entrain for home.
August	2	General parade of troops in Maritzburg at which his Excellency the Governor accords the officers and men the thanks of the Colony.

* * * * *

COST OF THE WAR

N. Cave in his "The High Human Cost of War" says:- The Bambata Rebellion of 1906 cost Natal RI,055,556.

* * * * *

Militia Headquarters
PIETERMARITZBURG
9th May 1907

M.O. 128 - AWARD OF MEDAL FOR NATAL NATIVE REBELLION, 1906

1. His Excellency the Governor directs it to be notified that His Majesty the King has been graciously pleased to approve the issue of a medal in recognition of Services rendered during the Native Rebellion in Natal in 1906.

2. The medal will, provided the claims are approved by His Excellency the Commander-in-Chief, be granted to all Officers, Warrant Officers, Non-Commissioned Officers and men of the Forces; to all Non-Attested Civilians serving in a Military capacity, and Nursing Sisters, who served in Natal and Zululand during the operations between the 11th February 1906, and 3rd August 1906, for a continuous period of not less than twenty days and who were in receipt of full pay for such period. Also to such Civilians, Native Chiefs, and others who rendered valuable service, and are approved by His Excellency the Governor.

3. A claps inscribed "1906" will be issued with this medal to every Officer, Warrant Officer, Non-Commissioned Officer, and man who served in Natal and Zululand during the operations betweens the 11th February 1906, and 3rd August 1906, for a continuous period of not less than fifty days, and who was in receipt of full pay for such a period.

4. In interpreting these rules the actual period of absence from duty on account of wounds or sickness directly attributable to service in the field will be allowed to count.

5. Commanding Officers will prepare nominal Rolls, in triplicate of the individuals entitled to the medal, and forward them as early as possible to the Chief Staff Officer, Militia Headquarters, Pietermaritzburg. A supply of printed forms of Rolls will be sent to each unit concerned.

6. The names of Officers and Warrant Officers will be entered in Order of rank, and those of Non-Commissioned Officers and men in alphabetical order.

7. In cases where it is known that individuals have served with more than one unit in the campaign, a note should be made on the roll, in the column provided for the purpose, showing the unit with which they previously served, and their ranks and regimental numbers therein.

8. The names of individuals who were discharged for misconduct, etc., and have so forfeited their claim to the medal, are to be included in the Rolls, their names being entered in red ink, and the cause of forfeiture stated in the last column.

9. The names of individuals who have become non-effective by death, transfer, or discharge should be inserted in the rolls in red ink, particulars as to cause of becoming non-effective to be stated in the column of remarks.

> H.T. Blew Major
> Chief Staff Officer
> Natal Militia

* * * * *

Annexures A, B and C are to be found in:-

MY VERULAM TROOPS - by Captain A.H. Garnet - Blamey.

Annexure A. (Being a copy of page 911 of the Natal Government Gazette of 26th June 1906)

MILITIA ORDERS
By Major-General Sir J.G. Dartnell, K.C.B., C.M.G., V.D. - Acting Commandamt of Militia

163. **DISTINGUISHED CONDUCT IN THE FIELD**

The Acting Commandant has great pleasure in publishing for generl information the names of the following Officers, Non-Commissioned Officers and Men who have distinguished themselves by deeds of gallantry in the Field:-

Captain E.G. Clerk, Royston's Horse, who, in the action at Nkandhla Forest, on the 3rd June 1906, when in an isolated position with a small number of men, was regourously attacked by overwhemling odds, and although severely wounded in both arms, continued to fight and rally his men, until such time as assistance arrived.

Lieutenant A.H.G. Blamey, Natal Mounted Rifles, in the action at Nkomo Hill, on the 5th May 1906, at the risk of his own life, rescued Corporal Arnott from a perilous situation. The latter had become detached from his troop, and, being unable to mount would certainly have fallen into the hands of the enemy but for Lieutenant Blamey's timely assistance.

Trooper W. Holmes, Royston's Horse, during the engagement at Nkandhla Forest, on the 3rd June 1906, displayed conspicuous gallantry. Although severely wounded in the thigh, he continued to support his squadron officer, and rendered valuable assistance at an extremely critical stage of the action.

Trooper C.W. Guest, Natal Police, on the night of the attack on the Police at Impanza River, 4th April 1906, dismounted at great risk to himself and rescued Trooper Emanuel, whose horse had fallen. Trooper Emanuel would undoubtedly have fallen into the enemy's hands but for Trooper Guest's gallant act.

S.R. Lawrenson, Captain
Staff Officer, Natal Militia.

* * *

Annexure B.

Col. E. Mace
Officer Commanding
Natal Mounted Rifles
Lords Ground
Old Fort Road
DURBAN

P.O. Mount Edgecombe
Natal
4th November 1953

Dear Col. Mace,

re: 1906 Zulu Rebellion and the 2 V.C's recommended: Captains Armstrong and Blamey, N.M.R.

Following on your request during our talk the other evening I am now setting out here details which I personally remeber having taken place at the time I was in the field during the 1906 Native Rebellion.

It is fairly common knowledge that the trouble started in 1906 at Byrne, near Richomnd, Natal, when the Natives in that district, upon being warned to assemble and pay their taxes, came fully armed with assagais and worked themselves up into an angry mood and murdered two of the tax collecting officials. The Native ring-leaders were arrested, brought to trial by court-martial, a squadron of Carbineers being on the spot at the time, and condemned to death, but the then Liberal Government in Britain interferred and delayed the execution. Most people felt at the time that this action created the idea in the Native mind that they were being supported by the British Government and encouraged them to extend their Rebellion and come out in force.

The Militia in Natal was immediately mobilised by Col. Bru-de-Wold, who was O.C. and dispersed to different parts of Natal and Zululand stationed at Fort Napier were not called upon to take any action as they were unpopular owing to the attitude of the British Government.

General Botha crossed the Berg with some Boer Commandos, and the Transvaal volunteer Regiments, viz: Imperial Light Horse and Transvaal Scottish, also came to Natal's assistance.

There are still many men alive who took part in this Rebellion and will have their tales to tell.

It will be of interest to you to know that the unpopular action of the British Liberal Government at that time was very much resented by the people of Natal and one incident which is worthy of mention is that the Union Jack was taken down in Durban and torn to pieces by the crowd. The feeling of the Country was that the Liberal Government was the cause of the Rebellion spreading as it did. As they were unsympathetic towards the Volunteer Regiments, the recommendations for the awards of the Victoria Cross to both Captain Garnet Blamey and Captain Robert Armstrong, did not receive sympathetic consideration.

> **Captain Garnet Blamey** was O.C. Verulam Troop NMR and was in a column under Col. Dymock of the Natal Police. On their way through Zululand, they were to join forces with other regeiments for the big drive. Blamey was sent up a hill with his troops to reconnoitre as the OC felt that there might be an ambush. He finally got to the top with his troop and saw the Natives very well hidden in long grass and they were immediatley attacked with assegais and guns. He gave the signal to retire and on looking back he saw Trooper Acutt surrounded by Natives and trying to mount his startled horse. The Natives were actually on the point of killing him, but Blamey galloped back scattering the Natives with his horse, Picked Acutt up right under the point of the assegais and threw him across his saddle and galloped off followed by a shower of missiles. Both escaped unjury by a miracle. The Natives were all around him as he galloped through with Acutt and he had to jump a line of Nongqai (Native Police) who were covering the troop and he and Acutt managed to get back to safety.
>
> Major or Col. Dymock of the Natal Police considered it was an outstanding act of valour on the part of Captain Blamey and he, with other officers, sent in a report to the

General Officer Commanding, (General Dartnell), recommending that he be awarded the Victoria Cross.

This recommendation was placed before the Governor of Natal, Col. Sir Henry McCallum, KCMG, who immediately forwarded it overseas. As the Governor's Colonial ADC, I went to see him off when he boarded the ship for England on the expiry of his office shortly after the rebellion ended. Sir Henry told me that he would personally see H.M. the King about the recommendation and hoped that the interview would bear fruit. Sir Henry was rather annoyed with me for not arranging for Blamey to be present to see him off, as he had especially requested his presence through his controller. He asked me to advise Blamey that he was seeing the King about the recommendation as upon the evidence before him it was an act of valour worthy of recognition. Capt. Garnet Blamey is still alive and is living at Umzumbi and would give you more details if you wanted them and also confirm what I have written.

Captain Robert Armstrong was also recommended for the Victoria Cross by Major Sam Campbell (Dr.) who was in charge of a column (including ox-wagons) proceeding to Thrings Post. Major Campbell was OC MI of the DLI and ordered Captain Robert Armstrong of the NMR, who had joined them at Gingindhlovu, to assist him. It was getting dark and Major Campbell sent Captain Armstrong ahead to find a suitable camping ground as they were in a nasty area with bush etc., surrounding the road. The Natives allowed the MI scouts to pass close by but when Captain Armstrong had proceeded about a mile along the road, he heard heavy firing from the column behind him. He subsequently told me at Mapumulo that he was in two minds as to what action to take, whether to carry out his orders or to return to assist "Little Dr." as he called Major Campbell.

He decided to go back immediately as he felt that the Natives would be amongst the wagons stabbing the cattle. He told me that he galloped right amongst the Natives, knocking some down and at the same time emptying his revolver. He had to jump the first line of the DLI lying down across the road and firing heavily, but landed safely. The oxen and wagons were in a turmoil and he immediately set to and straightened it out. The column had two cannons and they were firing grapeshot at point blank range. Captain Armstrong escaped unhurt but his saddle girth was cut by a bullet which slightly wounded his horse.

Captain Armstrong could have ridden off to safety but chose to return to the assistance of his fellows although by so doing he faced almost certain death from the Natives themselves and the Rexas Machine Gun and rifle fire up the road from the troops.

I can assure you from the information received from all those who were actually on the spot at the time, Captain Armstrong's behaviour was looked upon as a cold blooded deed of valour and but for this unmatched unsympathetic Liberal Government (damn them) our two officers would have received their awards.

Afterwards when Captain Armstrong joined us at Mapumulo and our three squadrons had rendezvoued, Col. Sparks spoke at our Mess dinner and proposed Captain Armstrong's health and stressed his valorous action and that he had been recommended for the Victoria Cross.

                              Yours sincerely,
                              W. CAMPBELL

* * *

Annexure C.

Until I received the above letter[2] from Lieutenant -Colonel E. Mace in November 1953, I had not had the slightest inkling that there had been any intention of recommending me for the bestowal of the Victoria Cross, the highest honour attainable by any soldier.

Learning of the recommendation forty-seven years afterwards came as a great surprise and a shock to me.

Even today, I cannot understand why I was never notified that His Excellency, Sir Henry McCullam, had desired to see me, for had I been notified, I should have spared no pains to obey what I should have looked upon as a command by the representative of His Majesty, King Edward VII., himself.

                        A.H.G. Blamey, Captain.
                        Natal Mounted Rifles,
                            "Muluka",
                            UMZUMBI.   30th March 1954

[2] This refers to a copy of the letter by W. Campbell quoted as Annexure "B".

THE MEDAL ROLL

The Medal Roll number shown with each Unit, was apparently allocated and recorded, by the Natal Militia Headquarters, as and when the returns were received by them.

* * *

AMABOMVU LEVY
No Clasps Issued
Supplementary Roll

Native	GELEGU KA NDBUYANA
	JOHANNES DHLAMINI
	MADUKUMBANA HHAHLA
	MAJIJI KA NOTSHETSHA
	MAKASANA KA MAWELI
	MANGWANN KA MVIKEYE:WA
	MAQATSHANA KA QOBO
	MASEKWANA KA MANQATSHA
	MASIPULA KA MBETEKAYI
	MATETA KA VOYI
	MAWENI KA KHLAHLA
	MELELI KA NDBUYANA
	MEYIJO KA SONYAMA
	NFULSHANA KA COBA
	MAYAMANA KA INKULUSTANA
	MZILAKAZI
	MZILAWEMBI KA NYONYANA
	NAVOVO KA HHAHLA
	NDMASENSE KA MOKO
	NDUNGE KA INIPINJAN
	NGUMBA KA MLONDOLOYI
	NYIKA KA NTENLTSHANA
	PITOLYA KA MASEKWANA
	SIBALO KA GILO
	SIDHLUVU KA BHUBA
	SIDINA KA MQAYANA
	SIGODO KA MAGEDANA
	SYIBAMPENI KA NINGWANE
	THOMAS MALINGA
	TSHAYINYONI KA MAHLEKA
	TSHEKWANE KA BHUBA
	TULWANE KA NQAQAVE

Total of 32 Awards:
With Clasps - Nil
No Clasps   - 32

AMAFUNZE TRIBE
No Clasps Issued
Roll No. 59

Pack Leaders
    BOBOKA
    GQWIZA
    GWAMBI
    HOBE
    JOBE
    KAYIKO
    KOSI
    MAGWIYANA
    MALAMBA
    MAQOYANA
    MCIJE
    MNYAKAYA
    MPUNYU
    MPUQE
    MQOMO
    MXOTSHWA
    NGIQE
    NGQUMBU
    NQOLA
    SIFILE

Total of 20 Awards:
With Clasps - Nil
No Clasps   - 20

BORDER MOUNTED RIFLES
With Clasp 1906
Roll No. 6

Lt.Col.	ARNOTT W.
Major	ARCHIBALD R.G.
	THRING F.L.
Capt/Adj.	GREER J.R.
Capt.	BROWN H.
	DALGARNO J.H.
	GORDON J.L.
	ROBINSON A.E.
Lt. QM	ARCHIBALD H.D.
Lt.	ALEXANDER W.
	FOSTER C.C.
	HOGG W.
	LONDON W.H.
	MATITZ S.S.
	PLATT C.
	WALKER J.
	WAY G.C.
RSM	HARRIS C.F.
RQMS	GARDNER G.A.
ORSM	LANGTON L.W.
SSM	GOLD C.J.
	SYMONS H.
	WALTON W.W.
	WHITFIELD F.S.
SQMS	ALBOROUGH W.S.
	GRAY E.J.
	GREER J.A.
	STONE A.K.
FQMS	ROBERTSON D.B.
SIM	HARRIS F.O.
Sgt.Cook	POSS E.
Sgt.Farr.	RINGO M.
	TAYLOR C.P.K.
Sgt.Sadl.	McCRYSTAL T.
Sgt.Tailor	
	McANDREW J.F.
Sgt.Trtr.	MOODY J.W.
O.R.Sgt.	FOSTER W.E.
Sgt.	BOSSE A.
	FRANKLIN G.P.
	GREER S.H.
	HULLEY G.D.
	HULLEY W.C.
	MACK A.R.
	MACK W.G.
	ROBINSON T.A.
	SHUTTLEWORTH A.H.
	TAYLOR H.A.
	TAYLOR W.J.
	WILL W.
	WILLSON C.H.
Cpl.	ADAMSON G.C.
	BAZLEY J.
	BROWN S.A.
	DEARLOVE T.C.
	FORTE W.F.
	FYNN H.T.

Cpl.	GRAHAM R.G.	Tpr.	GORDON W.D. McK.
	HARDMAN F.C.		GRANT P.H.
	JUSTICE R.C.		GRAY F.H.
	LAWSON A.E.		GROOM A.E.
	LUPKE J.		HAWKESWORTH H.E.
	MASON A.V.		HEPPES A.
	McKENZIE L.E.		HEPPES P.H.
	OOSTHUIS G.J.		HERBERTSON R.G.
	RAW H.M.		HOSKEN C.C.
	TAYLOR E.G.		HOUSTON D.D.
	THOMSON F.		HOWES T.W.
	WALTON G.		HUFFT W.F.A.
	WHITELAW W.W.		HULLEY J.R.
L/Cpl.	HINES T.H.		ISBISTER A.V.
	MAWDESLEY S.		ISBISTER W.C.
	STAFFORD R.E.H.		JOHNSTON G.H.
	VAN NIEKERK J.J.		KLUSENER F.
	WARDELL E.W.		LAIR G.
SS	GIDSKE K.R.		LANDERS J.C.
Tmptr.	BUCHANAN R.I.		LANGLANDS A.R.
	CLARKE A.W.		LAWSON C.
	McKENZIE N.B.		LAWSON G.
	PEMBROKE J.		LESLIE A.
Tpr.	ADCOCK J.		LESLIE W.B.
	ALBOROUGH E.		LISTER W.H.
	ALCOCK H.P.		MALCOLM D. McK.
	ANDERSON O.R.		MARITZ P.J.
	ARBUTHNOT E.N.		MARTIN W.E.
	ARCHER A.C.		McLAURIN J.W.M.
	BALLAND J.R.		McLEOD R.
	BAZLEY W.		MUNRO H.H.
	BEHRMANN F.H.C.		NOBLE H.
	BERNTS S.		NORRIS T.
	BLAMEY M.		OOSTHUIS F.W.
	BOUCHER J.H.		PAICE G.W.
	BRICKHILL A.G.		PALFRAMAN G.W.
	BRICKHILL F.S.		PEARCE B.J.W.
	BUTCHER W.J.		PEMBERTON W.T.
	CALF M.J.		PHIPSON B.J.
	CHRISTISON W.R.		PITOUT B.H.
	CHITTENDEN C.E.		RAW C.E.
	CLARKE G.D.		REID J.D.
	CLARKE R.		RESTON J.
	COMRIE W.		SALTER S.S.
	CONWAY T.J.		SHOOTER C.T.
	CORFE C.W.		SHRIVES G.C.
	CROCKER A.J.		SHRIVES H.
	CROCKFORD F.W.		SHUTTLEWORTH E.H.
	CROLL J.		SIMPSON J.
	DAWSON S.H.		SLATTER E.J.
	DOIDGE E.		SMALL A.J.
	DOWNS S.W.		SMITH D.F.
	DURNO G.		SMITH J.A.
	ELLIOTT R.M.		SPENCER W.E.
	ELLIS H.D.		STAFFORD A.E.
	ELLIS S.J.		STONE J.D.
	ERASMUS D.A.		STONE R.C.
	ERASMUS D.R.		SURRIDGE E.T.
	ERASMUS W.D.		SURRIDGE H.
	FANN N.		TAYLOR F.J.
	FISHER R.U.P.		TAYLOR H.V. (624)
	FLEE G.		TAYLOR H.V. (682)
	FORDER C.F.		THOMPSON F.R.
	FORDER M.H.		THOMPSON J.E.
	FOSTER W.H.		THOMSON W.O.
	FREEMEN H.		TOLMER H.T.
	FRUIN W.M.		TONNESON P.H.
	FURNISS T.		TUSTIN G.J.
	GELDART A.J.L.S.		TUSTIN J.F.
	GOLD A.R.		VAN DER MERRVE J.L.
	GOLD R.B.		VERMAAK H.
	GOLDSTONE H.		VETTER F.F.W.

Tpr.	VETTER P.
	WALKER R.
	WHITELAW F.S.
	WHITFIELD B.
	WHITFIELD G.
	WILKINSON W.H.
	WILL T.A.
	WILSON R.C.
	WILLSON A.
	WILLIAMS A.B.
	ZEITSMAN L.J.

No Clasps Issued

Capt.	AIKEN J.W.
Lt.	LUGG H.A.
SSM	MASON H.R.
Sgt.	ANDREASON A.H.E.
	ARCHIBALD H.D.
	HAAJEM K.
	STAPLETON T.
Cpl.	BJORSETH P.
	HAAJEM L.
	PEARCE J.
	SINCLAIR J.C.
SS	HARDOWIN E.
Tmptr.	BARKER W.A.
	GRIEVES A.
	KLUSENER W.
Tpr.	ANDREASON E.J.
	BARTH J.E.R.
	BATSTONE S.M.
	BJORSETH O.E.
	BULLEY W.
	CROCKER C.D.
	CROCKER W.J.
	CROOKES J.J.
	DEHRMANN H.
	EDWARDS J.K.
	FRANCIS V.E.
	GOLD L.
	KUCKUCK A.
	LILLEBO A.J.
	MANNING J.W.
	MILLER J.
	PEARCE E.J.
	SINCLAIR A.C.F.
	THORPE W.
	TRITTON E.
	VALDAL P.G.
	WATTS J.
	WEBER J.

Total of 251 Awards

With Clasps - 213
No Clasps - 38

The Regimental Numbers (although they do not appear on the medals) have been placed after the initials of both Troopers H.V. Taylor

CAPE MOUNTED RIFLEMEN
With Clasp 1906.
Roll No. 42

Capt.	HUMPHREY M.
Lt.	STOPFORD R.
Sgt.	ARMSTRONG J.G.
	DIXPEEK A.
	HINGESTON-RANDOLPH B.J.R.
Sgt.	ROBERTSON S.R.
	SCHIFF T.
Cpl.	BADDERLY F.C.J.
	CHARLS J.S.
	COPPINGER T.P.
	GORDON-GRAY G.
	HOWES G.W.
	OWEN W.
	SIKES J.H.
	WHITE A.H.
Pte.	AMES F.R.
	BISHOP C.F.
	BLACKADDER A.
	BOYD A.
	BURNE C.G.
	CLARK B.G.W.
	CLISDAL J.
	COOKE J.
	DICKMAN E.H.
	DOHERTY R.
	FOOTMAN J.
	GARRETT H.C.A.
	GLASGOW J.
	GOLD A.P.
	GRAY W.W.
	HARE R.
	HARPER R.H.
	HOLBROOK L.
	HOLLOWAY C.G.
	HULSE A.
	HULSEBERG E.A.
	KING F.S.R.
	LLOYD H.
	McCALLUM H.H.
	McDONALD J.
	MEARES C.H.N.
	MELLOR C.E.
	MORSE S.J.
	NEVILLE P. St.J.A.
	PETRE E.H.
	PINNOCK A.
	SCOTT CHARLES F.K.
	SCOTT DAVID
	SCOTT D.G.S.
	SEARLE M.J.R.
	TOMLIN G.
	TOOMEY R.M.
	TWYNAM J.
	VEREY C.
	WIEGARDT T.W.
	WILLIAMS B.S.
	WRIGHT O.R.
Native Tpr. 3rd Class	XIRA C.
Art.Native Drivers	ARTHUR
	BEZUIDENHUIT P.
	GANIA J.
	GEORGE R.
	GOOSEN A.
	GXUMEKA J.
	JERRIE
	JOSIAH
	MacDONALD I.
	MALHAAS
	MTUNA J.
	RAIB

Total of 70 Awards

With Clasps - 70
No Clasps - Nil

CHAPLAINS
With Clasp 1906
Roll Nos: 2, 45 & 59

Snr.
Chaplain   PENNINGTON G.E.
Chaplain   WILKINSON-RIDER W.
Hon.
Chaplain   ALLEN Revd. J.B.
            MILLS Revd. C.S.

No Clasps Issued

Chaplain   OSCROFT Revd. L.E.
            Nkandhla Town Guard
            TOSQUINET Revd. J.

Total of 6 Awards

With Clasps - 4

No Clasps - 2

CIVILIAN (NATAL) EMPLOYEES
No Clasps Issued
Roll No. 59 & Supplementary Roll

Sir   CHARLES SAUNDERS   KCMG
Hon.Mr.   CLAYTON W.F.
            HYSLOP T.
            MAYDON H.G.
            SMYTHE C.J.
            WATT T.
            WINTER D.
CL.   INGRAM F.
Mrs.   LANDSBURG
            POUNDER C.A.
No Rank   ADDISON R.H.
            ARMSTRONG G.W.
            BAMBRICK E.V.
            BARKLIE A.
            BASSAGE J.J.
            BOWNASS W.
            BRITTAIN T.
            BROWN H.M.
            BUSCOE C.
            CAMPBELL A.
            CHARLES
            COLENBRABDER B.
            CROSSLEY J.
            DAFFLE H.
            DIX F.H.
            DODD F.G.
            DOUGLAS A.
            DU TOIT
            FLORENCE W.
            FLYNN ANDERSON J.R.
            FRASER D.
            GRANT D.
            GRANT P.
            HARRINGTON A.E.
            HELLAWELL A.
            HIGNETT C.
            HOSKING W.H.
            JAMES S.
            JIM
            LONG F.W.
            McILLERON D.C.
            McKENZIE C.
            MDHLEMHLEM
            MILLER T.

No Rank   MILTON L.
            PLOWMAN G.F.
            POWELL W.J.
            RAMSAMMY
            RICHARDS J.
            ROUSE A.J.
            SAMUELSON S.O.
            SCHOESMITH G.
            SCHMIDT T.G.
            SMITH P.
            SMITH W.E.
            SNIBBLE T.
            SPENCER T.
            STIMSON G.J.
            WALTERS J.F.
            WEBBER A.W.
            WILLIAMS S.R.
            WITHYCOMBE W.A.
            WRIGHT R.S.
            TEATES T.

No Clasps Issued
Roll No. 59

Pack Leaders
            AYASAMI
            BAGWANDIN
            BASHAMAL H.
            BEGIZULU
            BELL M.
            BHEMIA
            BOUVRIE
            BOYCE B.
            CHENAPA
            DASHU
            DICK
            ELIAS
            ERRIGE G.
            FISH J.
            FRED
            GWEBULU
            HANS
            HLEGUVE
            JAN
            JOHAN
            JONASE
            KABIRA
            KAMYA
            KEHLA-ka-TSHIGI
            KUPPAN
            MADAFU
            MAFUTA
            MAGMINSEON D.
            MAHOMED
            MANTAI
            MARTENS
            MASOFILI
            MHLAGUWA ka MVEMBU
            MICHAEL
            MUHAMMED Y
            MUTHUVEEM
            MVUBU L.
            NCAKA
            NDEVU ka DOLWANE
            NKOSNA
            NOVAZI A.
            OTTO C.
            PATRICK
            PETER
            PETHAKUTU
            PEZENE
            PITIE ka NOZULELA

Pack Leaders
- PONI
- POONA
- PRETORIUS M.
- SAYSTER S.
- SILVAR
- SIMON
- SITENDE
- SKINNER J.
- SOLOMON P.
- SWART H.
- TOGWAYO
- UHLAGENE
- ULEY
- ULLBRICK S.
- UMTENISA
- UMTSHOGOBEZI
- VANUGH H.
- VERASAMMY
- VHY
- WILLIAM

Native Drivers
- BULIMAN
- IZWELAKE
- MPANGWA
- NDOSI

Total of 135 Awards

With Clasps - Nil

No Clasps - 135

Note: Mr. F.W. DIX was a Civilian Dispenser at the Queen Victoria Cottage Hospital Eshowe at this time. The only Dispenser to qualify for the medal.

DOCTORS (NATAL CIVILIAN EMPLOYEES)
No Clasps Issued
Roll No. 59

Dr.
- FENTON J.
- FLOOK H.S.
- REYNOLDS H.S.
- SAVAGE W.A.

Total of 4 Awards

With Clasps - Nil

No Clasps - 4

1st DUNDEE BOROUGH RESERVES
No Clasps Issued
Roll No. 33

Chief Leader THORROLD W.
Leader MEEK W.E.
QM Sub-Leader HEAD H.J.
Sub-Leader BILLINGE C.
           WOODLAND G.F.
Sgt. BOYLE A.R.
     MAGOR W.G.
Cpl. ARCHBELL W.R.
     De VALENCE R.P.
     GRIFFIN B.G.

Cpl.
- HARBER W.L.
- TATHAM A.H.
- TRAVERS E.L.
- WILLIAMS G.H.

Pte.
- ABRAHAM C.
- BAXTER H.M.
- BROKENSHA O.
- COUPAR A.
- CRACKNELL E.G.
- CRESWELL D.R.
- CUNNINGHAM J.S.W.
- DOIGE W.H.
- DOUGLAS A.
- FURBER W.H.
- GRIFFIN A.A.
- GUTRIDGE V.F.
- HARRIS C.
- HASTIE W.
- KRUGER H.J.C.
- LENNOX J.G.
- LEPPARD J.
- McGIRK M.A.
- McPHAIL D.M.
- MITCHELL B.
- WILLIAMS C.A.

Total of 35 Awards

With Clasps - Nil

No Clasps - 35

DUNDEE DISTRICT RESERVES
No Clasps Issued
Roll No. 52

Chief Leader Uys D.C.
Leader VAN RENSBURG N.J.
       VAN TONDER A.J.
Adj. VERMAAK P.R.N.
Sub-Leader DAVEL J.J.
           VAN ROOYEN S.C.
QMS KONING W.A.
Sgt. BOTHA J.
     MARITZ S.
Cpl. GRABE F.J.
     HOGG P.
     KEMP J.S.
     LAAS F.C.
     LANDMAN J.
     VAN DEN BERG L.J.
     WOHLITZ H.
Pte. BOSHOFF J.H.F.
     BRITZ G.P.
     CHIOLIE J.
     COLLER A.
     CROSS T.
     CRONJE P.
     CRONJE P.C.
     DE BRUIN P.W.
     DEKKER D.C.
     DOHNE A.C.
     DOHNE J.L.
     DOHNE J.M.
     EGNER J.
     FERREIRA R.J.
     HATTING M.
     HEDDER A.
     HEDDER E.

Pte.	JONES G.A.		**DURBAN LIGHT INFANTRY**

Pte.   JONES G.A.
       JORDAAN G.J.
       JORDAAN J.
       KEMP F.J.
       KEMP J.
       KEMP W.
       KOK F.R.
       KOK G.J.
       MARAIS B.G.
       MARAIS L.F.
       MOOLMAN W.H.
       MURRAY T.
       NANDE W.S.
       NEL I.
       NEL J.
       NEL J.T.
       ODE A.R.
       PELSTER C.P.
       PROZISKY E.
       SCHEEPERS M.J.
       SITTLAAR I.
       TALJAARD W.A.
       VAN TONDER A.J.
       VAN TONDER M.
       VERMAAK H.
       WEBB T.
       WYK A.L.
       ZEITSMAN J.F.
       ZEITSMAN J.S.

Total of 62 Awards

With Clasps - Nil

No Clasps   - 62

Note; Pte. A.R. ODE appears to be intended for Audie. Pte. W.S. NANDE appears to be intended for Naude.

DUNNS SCOUTS, INTELLIGENCE SERVICE
With Clasp 1906
Roll No. 12

Tpr.   DELANGE B.
       DELANGE H.
       DUNN F.
       DUNN G.
       DUNN H.J.
       DUNN R.
       DUNN S.W.
       DUNN V.
       GIELINK J.
       McDONALD G.
       McLOCKLAND F.
       NUNN C.
       NUNN G.
       NUNN H.
       NUNN J.
       NUNN R.
       ROKIE J.
       ROKIE W.
       THRING F.
       TOOLEY F.

Total of 20 Awards

With Clasps - 20

No Clasps - Nil

DURBAN LIGHT INFANTRY
With Clasp 1906
Roll No. 29

Lt.Col.   WYLIE J.S.
Major   CAMPBELL S.G.
            NICOL J.
Brvt.Maj.   MOLYNEUX G.
Capt/Adj.   CLARKSON C.F.
Capt.   ALEXANDER W.
            BURNE W.L.
            GALBRAITH R.C.
            GOULDING R.L.
            HENDERSON W.P.M.
            NICOLSON J.H.
Lt.Paym.   WORMAN A.E.
Lt.   ARBUTHNOT W.S.G.R.
            BUCKLE W.F.
            BURNE G.R.
            CLEMMANS E.H.
            GREEN A.E.
            HOOD J.
            LAGERWALL F.
            McCUBBIN T.
            McWILLIAM C.N.
            MOLYNEAUX L.
            NEILSON V.J.
            NUTTALL E.E.
            OWLES D.C.
RSM   FORBES A. DCM
WO Band
Master   GRANT T.J.
Col.Sgt.   EALES A.
            KETTLE C.
            LAUTH R.
            PREECE A.I.
            POISSON L.C.
            SHAND A.
            TURNER E.G.
            WRIGHT J.
Drum Maj.   WHITEAR H.E.
S/Sgt.   MILLETT H.S.O.
            REYNOLDS G.R.
            STONIER C.A.
QMS   PARRY E.C.
Sgt.Armr.   SELLARS A.
Sgt.Farr.   GREENSLADE W.
Sgt.Paym.   THOMAS F.R.
Sgt.   BRINKWORTH R.
            BUCHANAN J.R.
            BURNE G.E.
            CHEESMEN E.M.
            COLLINS C.T.
            CUMMING G.
            DOWSE F.J.
            DURNO L.
            EDWARDS F.J.
            GILLMORE W.D.
            HARRIS J.H.
            HARROLD H.
            HARVEY A.E.
            HORNE W.
            JOHNSON J.E.
            KERR J.
            LINN W.A.
            LORIMER R.M.
            LOW F.W.
            MILES C.
            MILLS T.
            NOURSE A.D.
            PARFITT T.

Sgt.	SHACKLETON E.	Pte.	BAKER J.J.
	SIMMONDS E.		BAKER S.F.
	SMITH F.J.		BALLANTINE A.S.
	STRIDE P.		BALLARD V.P.
	THOMSON W.		BANWELL H.T.
	TILL R.J.		BARAGWANATH E.
	WELCH W.E.		BARNES J.H.
	WELLS A.T.		BARTLETT W.H.
	WILLIAMSON W.		BEAMISH F.
	WILLIS J.M.		BERNDT H.
Cpl.	ARNOLD E.H.		BICKNELL D.
	ATKINSON A.B.		BIRSS C.G.
	ARTHUR G.		BOUCHIER P.
	BEATON G.		BOWMAN H.
	BRANDER G.A.		BOYLE H.J.
	BURNE J.O.		BRADSHAW F.
	COWIE J.		BRADY A.C.
	DAVID F.		BRAND C.
	DEW G.		BRAND G.
	DIXON W.G.		BRASH J.
	DOWNIE T.H.		BRERETON G.S.
	DOWSETT S.G.		BRODERICK H.
	DUNCAN W.G.		BROOK C.A.
	EVANS T.J.		BROOMHEAD A.
	FAINE G.		BROUGHTON T.W.
	FIELD F.J.		BROWN A.E.
	FLETCHER J.		BROWN G.F.
	FREETH J.F.		BROWN G.G.
	GRAY C.		BROWN J.
	HATHORN J.A.		BUCHANAN W.
	HAZELL T.R.		BUDD G.F.
	HOSKINS W.K.		BUDGEON J.W.
	KEITH M.W.		BULLOUGH F.
	KETTLE E.E.		BURKE T.
	KING H.E.		BURNE A.E.
	LLOYD S.E.		BURNE C.H.
	MATHIAS W.		CAMPBELL E.D.
	McDONALD J.		CAPELL H.E.
	McQUEEN H.A.		CARR M.
	MORRILL T.		CARR R.T.
	OLSEN O.B.		CARTNELL E.
	RAINBOW H.J.		CARTWRIGHT A.B.
	REED L.		CARTWRIGHT W.B.
	RICHMOND A.C.		CASS R.
	RIDLEY H.E.		CATTS A.G.
	RUMNEY C.		CECIL E.B.
	SMITH W.J.		CHAPMAN W.J.
	SPARNON E.		CHERRY M.
	STAFFORD E.J.		CHRISTIAN R.H.
	STEPHENSON J.J.		CLARENCE C.L.
	TOMLINSON A.		CLARENCE E.
	TRAYNOR D.		CLEAVER T.
	UTTON W.P.		CLEE E.
	WATSON A.S.		CLIFTON V.
	WATSON H.		CLOUGH J.
	WOOD C.H.		COBB D.
	WOOTON S.		COCHRANE J.L.
L/Cpl.	JOLLY J.		COGHILL C.
	KETTLE W.		COLE H.G.
Pte.	ADAMS E.		COLES H.
	ADAMS H.		COLQUHOUN J.
	ALEXANDER T.		CONNOR J.
	ALLEN G.		CONSTABLE J.
	ALLEN J.C.		COOK R.
	ALLEN T.		COULDREY F.J.
	ANDERSON A.		COUTTS W.H.
	ANDERSON A.C.		CRAIG W.
	ANDREWS A.E.		CRAWFORD W.
	ARMOUR J.		CULLEN C.
	ASSERSOHN J.		CUMMING D.G.
	ATKIN E.		CURRIE J.M.
	BAIN C.		CURRIE R.R.

Pte.	CUTHBERTSON W.	Pte.	HAMMOND W.
	DANIELS G.W.		HARRIS F.G.
	DAVIS T.		HARRISON A.
	DAY H.		HARRISON H.J.
	DELLIS A.		HARTOP F.C.
	DELLIS J.		HEYES J.
	DICKASON L.		HAYWARD H.G.
	DICKSON G.E.		HEATH A.E.
	DILLON T.		HEAVEY W.
	DIXON W.J.		HENDERSON W.
	DOBLE G.H.P.		HERBERT J.
	DOBLE J.W.		HILL W.A.
	DODWELL E.		HOBSON C.B.
	DONNE G.E.		HODGKINSON W.
	DOUGLAS W.		HOLLAND A.C.
	DOVE F.H.		HOPSON E.
	DOWSE A.G.		HORROCKS J. (1092)
	DRISCOLL S.J.		HORROCKS J. (1703)
	DRUMMOND A.		HORSLEY J.
	DUBREY W.J.		HUDSON E.
	DUKE H.		HUDSON M.
	DUNSTON S.		HUGHES J.
	EALES S.		HUMPHREY H.A.
	EDGSON G.E.		HURLEY A.
	EDWARDS C.B.		HUTCHINSON W.B.
	ENNION W.H.		HYDE J.
	ENNIS P.H.		INGRAM P.J.
	EVANS J.P.		JACK C.D.
	EWAN J.		JACKSON A.
	FAINE H.B.		JACKSON F.D.
	FAIRBAIRN J.J.W.		JACKSON H.
	FEARN C.G.		JACKSON J. (1643)
	FERGUSON D.		JACKSON J. (1984)
	FERGUSON J.		JACOBSON W.R.
	FINNEGAN T.		JENKINS C.E.
	FITZGERALD M.		JENKINS T.A.
	FLORENS W.		JENKINSON H.
	FORBES J.R.		JESSHOP E.W.
	FOSTER A.		JOHNSON G.
	FOSTER E.J.		JOHNSON P.H.
	FOSTER J.		JOHNSTON W.J.
	FOX E.P.		JONES C.E.
	FOYN H.		JONES H.
	FRANCIS W.		JONES S.A.
	FRASER A.		JONES W.
	FRIER W.		JOSEPHSON H.
	FRISBY E.		KEAST W.J.
	FROSTICK H. (1152)		KEIT N.
	FROSTICK H. (1271)		KERNS M.
	FRY D.		KEYTON B.
	GADSBY R.		KILPATRICK W.
	GALTRY R.		KING N.
	GARNER H.		KING S.E.
	GAULD H.		KING T.
	GAVIN J.W.		KIRK W.
	GILTINAN D.		KJODE J.
	GRACE G.C.		KNIGHT J.
	GRAHAM W.		KNOX H.
	GRANGER R.		LAGERWALL O.
	GRANT W.E.		LALAND F.D.
	GREEN F.K.		LANDMEAD S.
	GREGORY W.		LANGTON N R.
	GREYSON A.L.		LAVARACK F.
	GRICE J.H.		LAVERY A.
	GRIFFITHS J.		LAWRENCE W.
	GRIGGS W.		LAZARUS J.B.
	GWILLAM A.E.		LAZARUS L.E.
	GWILLAM W.S.		LCE C.
	HADEN A.L.		LEE T.
	HALE P.		LEE W.
	HALL G.H.		LEES W.
	HAMILTON J.		LEESON L.

Pte.	LEWIS E.W.	Pte.	RASMUSSEN V.E.
	LINDLEY L.R.		EAWLINSON A.E.
	LITTLE W.B.		RAWLINSON W.
	LLOYD W.H.		RECHENBERG J.
	LORIMER P.J.		REDMOND J.
	LOUDON T.		REINERT J.
	LYNE J.H.		RESSEL P.G.
	MACINTOSH R.		RICHES E.
	MAJOR W.H.		RIGBY J.
	MAPLE J.E.		RITCHIE E.R.E.
	MARA A.J.		RITCHIE W.
	MARSH A.C.		ROBBINS H.
	MARSHALL J.		ROBBINS W.F.
	MARSHALL R.		ROBERTS A.
	MARTIN A.		ROBERTS A.B.
	MASSEY V.A.		ROBERTSON J.
	MATTHEWS A.W.		ROBERTSON W.
	MATTHEWS R.		ROBERTSON W.R.
	MAY J.		ROWAN S.
	McDONALD A.		ROWE B.H.
	McDOWELL J.F.		SAUNDERS R.
	McFADYEN J.		SAYERS W.T.
	McGILL J.H.		SCHAFFER W.
	McGIVARY A.		SCOTT V.
	McINTYRE J.W.		SCOTT W.
	McLEAN A.		SELLARS C.
	McKENZIE D.		SELLARS D.
	McKINNEY W.		SENTER T.W.
	MERRY A.		SHEARER J.
	MILLER F.		SHEPHARD J.H.
	MILLS F.		SHEPPARD F.A.
	MITCHELL A.		SHERWOOD W.H.
	MOORE W.		SHORT T.
	MORLEY D.		SIME G.
	MORRIS G.		SIMPSON C.G.
	MORRIS L.C.		SINCLAIR G.D.
	MORRISON W.		SIVERTSEN S.
	MUNDY W.		SKONE W.
	MUNT G.H.B.		SMITH C.W.
	MURPHY P.O.		SMITH E.M.
	MYLES G.		SMITH H.
	NICHOLS J.E.		SMITH H.J.
	NICHOLLS R.C.		SMITH J.
	NOBLE A.		SMITH R.
	NORCOTT A.		SMITH T.
	NUTTALL W.		SMITH T.F.
	ODGERS J.H.		SPENCE E.R.
	OSBORNE J.		SPILLER C.
	PALMER C.J.		SPIRES E.
	PALMER S.		STEPHEN H.
	PARRY E.		STERLING F.
	PATRICK J.		STEVENSON J.W.
	PAXTON H.R.		STEWART J.A.
	PAYNE H.		STUART D.
	PAYNE J.		STUART J.C.
	PECKETT A.		SULLIVAN D.
	PEDERSEN T.		SULLIVAN E.
	PEPPER H.C.		SWANNEPOEL W.
	PETCH F.		SWINTON J.R.
	PETCH O.		SYKES S.L.
	PETERS J.		TAIT A.
	PETERS L.		TAYLOR A.
	PETERS W.P.		TAYLOR W.
	POLLECUTT C.H.		THOMPSON C.
	PRICE P.		THOMPSON G.
	PRICE S.L.		THOMPSON G.E.
	PUGH R.		THOMPSON J.
	PURVIS W.O.		THOMPSON L.
	RADCLIFF T.		THOMPSON R.
	RAFTER C.		THOMPSON T.T.
	RAPSON M.		TIERNEY A.N.
	RASMUSSEN J.S.		TIERNEY G.J.

Pte.	TIMPSON J.		Pte.	CROSSLEY E.H.W.
	TOMLINSON L.C.			DALLAS D.M.
	TRUEMAN S.			DOLAN F.
	VICKERMAN M.D.			DROMARD W.L.
	VINGOE J.			ESTON S.
	VOWLES F.B.			ETHERDEN J.F.
	WADE P.C.			FREEMAN G.
	WALLIS A.			FREEMAN T.
	WALTERS G.R.			GEORGE R.
	WARD C.			GIFKINS W.H.
	WARD R.			HARDIE T.
	WARNER C.A.			HARTLEY W.
	WARNER J.			HODGES H.
	WATSON T.			HULLSTOM A.
	WEAR C.J.			ILLINGWORTH E.
	WEBB H.N.			IRELAND J.
	WEDDERBURN E.G.			ISHERWOOD W.
	WESTON A.G.			JACKSON F.
	WESTON R.			JACKSON N.
	WETTERGREEN P.			JACOBS J.M.
	WHEELER R.			JOHNSON G.
	WHITE J.			LARCEN C.
	WHITEFORD W.			LOADER J.
	WHYTE J.			LOWE J.H.
	WIGGETT C.S.			LUCAS C.
	WILLIAMS A.			LUDERS F.A.
	WILLIAMS F.			LUND C.
	WILLIAMS W.			MACKAY D.
	WILLIS S.G.			MACKRORY F.
	WILLSTEAD W.			MADDEN F.
	WILSON T.			MARILLIER G.E.
	WINSOR H.			MAY H.P.
	WINSOR H.H.			McKECHNIE C.G.
	WOOD B.D.			McKENZIE A.
	WOODS W.A.			McLEOD A.
	WRIGHT F.			MITCHELL S.
	WRIGHT J.R.			MITCHELMORE W.A.
	WRIGHT R.			MOORE F.W.W.
	WRIGHT W.			MYER M.
	YOUNG J.C.			NOTTAGE T.H.
				ODGERS B.
No Clasps Issued				PEACOCK H.S.
				PEARCE A.C.
Capt.	JUDD J.S.			PETCH H.
Lt.	GARDNER J.			POWELL F.
SIM	SIGURDSON O.			PULFORD F.
Sgt.	NOLAN I.W.			PULVENIS M.
	SCOTT T.			PYM H.M.T.
Cpl.	COLLINS A.			PYNE S.W.
	HUDSON W.			RITCHIE J.L.
	LAGERWALL B.R.			ROBB G.
	LAW E.E.			RUSSELL G.
	McLEOD R.			RYAN P.
	MIDDLESBOROUGH J.R.W.			SHORT J.
Pte.	AIKMAN G.			SHUFFLEBOTHAM J.
	ANDERSON A.J.			STEWART A.
	AVERY S.M.			SUTHERLAND P.
	BAKER C.			THIEL G.
	BARICHIEVY A.W.			TUCKER L.B.
	BERRY F.			WILSON J.
	BITCON J.C.			WRAGG G.H.
	BOND W.D.			YOUNG T.
	BOURK W.E.			
	BOYD C.			
	BROMLEY W.J.			
	BROWN E.			
	BROWN F.W.			
	BROWN H.			
	BRUNYEE R.			
	CLARK A.C.			
	CLARK G.			
	COLE J.			
	COMPRERE F.			

Total of 632 Awards

With Clasps - 539

No Clasps - 93

Note: Sgt. J.M. WILLIS has two medals with clasps issued to him. The Regimental Nos. (Although they do not appear on the medal have been placed after the initials of those whose rank, initials and surnames are the same.

DURBAN MILITIA RESERVES
No Clasps Issued
Roll No. 49

Chief Leader	CHIAZZARI N.W.	Pte.	BUCKLE H.W.
Leader	BULLEY R.E.		BULLIVANT W.
	EDWARDS E.T.		BURNESS J.
	GILLESPIE H.M.		CAPEYRON H.
	LAW G.R.F.		CARMONT S.A.
	MARTINEAU H.R.		CASLEY H.
	SILBURN H.		CHALSTY T.F.
	SPARKS A.		CHAPLIN P.J.
	STRIKE J.R.		CHAPMAN R.B.
	TOWNSEND A.		CHISHOLM W.
S/M	LEAF-WRIGHT J.		CLARK P.J.
QMS	STEPHENSON F.J.		COLES B.G.
Sgt.	AITCHESON A.M.		COWLEY B.P.
	BEST J.		CUPPAGE A.H.
	BIRT A.R.W.		CURRIE A.W.
	CAPSTICK T.B.		DALE E.E.
	CROWLEY E.		DANIELSEN G.
	EDMONDS G.C.		DAUBER F.I.
	GIRLING F.M.		DENNANT P.E.
	HALL F.B.		DEUCHARS J.G.
	JONES G.		DOVE J.
	KING S.		DOWNIE F.
	KLAPKA A.C.		DRYSDALE F.
	MacDOUGALL J.		DUNCAN T.G.
	MORRIS C.J.		DUNNE W.A.
	ROWLAND C.E.		EASTERBROOKE S.
	SHEPPARD F.W.D.		EATON J.
	WOOD W.S.M.		ELLINGTON E.A.
Cpl.	CAMPTILL P.		FAYLE A.T.
	FINDLAY H.A.		FENNER F.
	HEY G.		FERGUSON R.E.
	HOWDEN J.P.W.		FINCHER C.
	NEEDHAM J.		FINNEY F.A.
	REID J.T.		FLINT G.A.
	ROBERTSON W.		GALBRAITH R.
	SALBERG E.T.		GEE J.H.
	SCOTT A.		GOLDIE O.B.
	SHAW A.R.		GOLDMAN W.B.
	STANDEN H.		GRICE L.C.
	TAYFIELD M.		HAMBLIN H.
	WEBB R.E.		HAMILTON H.
	WHITE J.D.		HANBURY S.S.
	WRIGHT J.		HARRISON L.G.
	YOUNG C.O.H.		HENDERSON A.E.E.
Pte.	ADAMS E.S.		HENDERSON T.
	ANDERSON W.A.		HENDERSON W.D.
	ARNESON C.J.		HENRY J.
	ASHLEY F.C.		HILLS W.
	BAILLIE J.		HIRST F.
	BALLARD E.H.		HOOPER E.P.
	BARTRAM H.A.		HUNT C.G.
	BAXTER I.J.		JOHNSON J.
	BAXTER W.A.		KEENE A.E.
	BEATON J.		KELLOCK A.H.
	BECKETT A.		KELLY C.
	BEGGS J.R.		KING J.A.
	BERNARD G.		LARCHE E.
	BESWICK F.		MacDONALD D.
	BEVERIDGE A.		MASON O.T.
	BISHOP G.S.		McCRACKEN T.
	BODEN C.E.		McLAREN G.
	BRADBROOK F.		McLEAN E.
	BREY C.A.		MILLS R.
	BRINTON J.		MITCHELL J.
	BROWN J.		MOCKETT A.
	BUCHANAN D.		MORRISON R.A.
	BUCKLE B.C.		MUNRO C.
			NEEDHAM T.
			NEILSON W.
			NICHOLLS E.H.
			NICOLL V.L.
			NURSE R.

Pte.	PATTERSON O.G.	Sub-	
	PEARSON J.	Leader	LAWRENCE J.
	PECHEY R.C.		MARITZ F.
	PETIT G.B.		WINTER A.H.
	PIRIE A.	QM	COOKE A.O.
	POTTER C.F.	Sgt/Majo.	HEENAN C.R.
	POYNTON R.	QM.Sgt.	DIBBLE F.W.
	PRATT F.	Farr.Sgt.	SIMPSON H.
	PRINCE L.P.	Sgt.	ACUTT C.R.C.
	REEVES W.		AIRTH J.A.
	RENAUD J.		HATTING J.S.
	RENAUD J.L.		HORNER F.
	RICHMOND E.		RALFE M.E.J.
	RIDGWAY J.V.		SCHMIDT C.F.
	RILLIE P.	Cpl.	BEYERS M.
	RIPLEY E.E.		BROWN F.
	RIPLEY H.G.W.		DIBBIN D.C.M.
	RITCHIE C.C.		HATTINGH J.M.
	ROBERTS J.		KERR J.
	ROBERTSON W.K.		MEYER I.J.
	ROSS G.		MULCAHY H.H.
	SAKER E.S.		PORRILL C.
	SALTER S.B.		POTTERILL A.E.
	SCOTT W.W.		SMITH H.P.
	SEALY B.	Tpr.	ACUTT C.S.C.
	SEALY C.V.		ACUTT R.C.
	SEWELL P.		ANDERSON A.
	SINCLAIR R.		ANGUS J.
	SIMS A.G.		BENNETT T.R.
	SLEE G.B.		BEYERS C.
	SMITH C.		BLAKEMAN R.
	SMITH J.		BOSHOF G.R.
	SNYMAN J.N.H.		BOSHOFF J.N.
	SPARKS A.C.		BOWMAN G.I.
	STEWART A.C.		BOWMAN G.I.
	STILES R.		BRICKHILL G.
	STORM J.		BROUGHTON B.D.
	STRIKE T.M.		BURMISTON E.T.
	SWALES C.H.		BUTTEMER E.
	THORPE C.		CASTELYN W.
	TOBIAS J.		CAUTHERLEY E.
	TONKIN L.		CHADWICK J.M.K.
	TREHAIR C.T.		FOULKES H.E.J.
	TREHAIR E.		GEVERS H.C.
	TREHAIR J.W.		GREEN H.
	TUNNER M.D.		GULDENPFENNING J.H.
	VONCK W.		GULDENPFENNING J.H.
	WAKEFIELD J.H.		HAMILTON J.
	WASSERMAN D.		HANDLEY F.W.
	WATSON W.A.		HASSALL F.P.
	WEBB B.		HATTINGH J.H.
	WILKES G.L.		HATTINGH W.C.
	WILKS J.A.		HEATH M.R.
	WILLY A.		HELLERLE H.
	WILSON E.W.		HINDLE F.L.
			HOLMES C.
			HORNER F.
			HOSKING H.H.
			HOUSTON J.
			HOWELL H.
			JACOBI A.
			JEWITT H.
			JEWITT T.
			KIRKLAND J.
			LANG W.H.
			LINDSAY F.
			LOMBAARDT A.
			LOUWRENS C.L.
			MAJOR H.C.
			McGRATH D.
			MOOR C.
			MOOR D.R.

Total of 194 Awards

With Clasps - Nil

No Clasps - 194

1st ESTCOURT MILITIA RESERVES
With Clasp 1906
Roll No. 40

Chief		
Leader	HENDERSON A.F.	CMG
Leader	BRIDSON G.	
	LYNDON W.	
	VAN DER MERWE C.J.	

Tpr.	OOSTHUIZEN P.J.		Tpr.	CLYNE G.W.
	OWEN D.J.			DUCKHAM E.
	PORRILL M.J.			GRIFFIN H.
	RALFE C.			HARRIS G.
	RANDLES C.C.			HUTCHINSON W.J.
	REEVES C.M.			KIRKLAND C.H.
	ROBBERTSE J.B.			LEE J.S.
	ROHRS O.			LEPPARD H.
	SCHEEPERS B.G.			LOADER A.
	SCHEEPERS M.J.			MENNE V.T.
	SCHEEPERS N.B.			MISSELHORN H.W.
	SCHOEMAN J.			MUIR J.
	SEWELL C.			NEL G.C.
	SNYMAN C.F.			PERRY W.
	SNYMAN L.Y.			RENNIE W.
	STEVENS W.S.			ROBERTS G.S.
	STEWART H.			SHEARER W.J.
	STYLES R.			STEEL J.B.
	SUTTON H.W.			STIEGER J.M.H.
	TAYLOR C.W.			STIEGER M.L.
	VAN DER MERWE A.P.			TILLETT J.
	VAN DER MERWE C.F.			TYLER G.H.
	VAN DER MERWE G.B.			UNSWORTH H.
	VAN DER MERWE H.J.			VAN ROOYEN G.T.
	VAN DER MERWE I.M.			VAN ROOYEN H.
	VAN DER MERWE J.R.			VERMAAK P.H.
	VAN DER WESTHUIZEN G.J.			WALKER R.
	WALDWICK J.F.			WILSON T.
	WICKENS W.J.			YOUNG G.
	WILSON J.			
	WOODS H.			

Total of 42 Awards

No Clasps Issued

With Clasp - Nil

Tpr.   BRAMMER G.

No Clasps - 42

        BROMLEY J.W.
        BUTTON E.
        EDDIE J.G.

2nd GREYTOWN RESERVES
With Clasps 1906
Roll No. 41

        FRISCKE T.R.
        JANSEN P.W.
        McDULING R.C.
        NEWTON H.

Cpl.   DUFF A.A.

Total of 1 Award

        OOSTHUIZEN J.N.
        POTGIETER G.C.
        SPINK J.
        TORKINGTON R.H.
        TURPIN C.A.

With Clasp 1

HIS EXCELLENCY THE GOVERNOR AND PERSONAL STAFF.
With Clasp 1906
Roll No. 1

Total of 118 Awards

With Clasps - 105

H/E Col.   Sir H.E. McCALLUM R.E.
Major   H.E. WALTER
              3rd Btn Lincolnshire Regt.

No Clasps - 13

No Clasps Issued

1st GREYTOWN RESERVES
No Clasps Issued
Roll No. 41

Mr.   A.J. HEDGELAND
        Civilian. Private Secretary
        to the Governor.

Leader   CADLE G.E.
Sub-
Leader   ZUNCKEL O.M.
QMS   ARBONS A.
Sgt.   BECKER T.F.
          HUBER C.A.
Cpl.   BROWN L.L.
          CARTER A.
          SHORT J.
          STIEGER W.
Tpr.   ALBERS H.
          BINGHAM G.A.
          BLACK W.H.
          BROOK C.R.

Total of 3 Awards

With Clasps - 2

No Clasps - 1

IMPERIAL OFFICERS
No Clasps Issued
Roll No. 56

Major	CROOKSHANK C.W.		No Rank	HODSON J.
	Royal Engineers			MARE W.W.
Capt.	LIPSETT L.J.			NENIMARCH T.H.
	Royal Irish Regiment			ZINEKE
Lt.	MAGILL H.P.			
	L.N. Lanc Regiment			
Lt.	ORDE-BROWNE G. St.J.			
	Royal Garrison Arty			

Total of 4 Awards

With Clasp - Nil

No Clasps - 4

Note: to the above names could perhaps be added that of Major H.E. WALTER, 3rd Bn. Lincolnshire Regt; however his name appears on the roll of "His Excellency the Governor and Personal Staff".

INDIAN STRETCHER BEARER CORPS
No Clasps Issued
Roll No. 24

S/M	GANDHI M.K.
Sgt.	JOSHI H.I.
	MEDH S.B.
	SHELAT U.M.
Pte.	ADOHASING
	ALWAR
	APPALSAMY
	BOMAYA
	COOPOOSAMY
	JAMALUDDIN
	KHAN M.
	KISTAMA
	KUNJI
	MAHOMED
	MAHOMED E.
	MOOT H.
	PARBHU H.
	POOTI N.
	SHEIK D.M.
	SHEIK M.

Total of 20 Awards

With Clasps - Nil

No Clasps - 20

INTELLIGENCE SERVICE
With Clasp 1906
Roll No. 14, 23 & 58

Chief Intelligence Officer	HOSKING E.J.B.
Sgt/Inter.	HOSKING E.C.
Tpr.Guide	WEIR W.A.
Tpr.	FRIEND L.
	OTTO R.J.P.
Native Scout	GEORGE KA NONGAMULANA
	GWABABA KA NONGAMULANA
	MBONI KA NONGAMULANA
	NOHLOVU KA NONGAMULANA
	TSHETSHA KA NONGAMULANA
No Rank	ASTRUP J.
	BAYEKANA
	GEORGE

No Clasps Issued

S/Maj.	MOLIFE J.
Chief	MKIZE J.
	MVELI
	NYANTSHI
	NYONIGEYWA
	SIBINDI
Sgt.	XABA S.
Nat.Cons.	DWALANA
	JIMPOQO
	MCOQIBELO
	NGUNA
Tpr.	HORSLEY R.
Tpr/Guide	LONGCAST H.W.
No Rank	BEPE
	BOB
	DIBI
	GUMEDE
	JONAS
	MANGALISO KAMBULI
	MANTSHONGO
	MAQULWANA
	MATEW
	MKUKWANE
	MKWANAZE
	NADAWOMNITI
	NDKUYAKE
	NONDELA
	SEULA
	SHWILI
	SLMGOYELI
	SOLOMON
	TOTO
	TUNYI

Total of 51 Awards

With Clasps - 17

No Clasps - 34

Note: the medals to the following three chiefs were re-engraved medals:
Mveli, Nyonigeywa, Sioindi

KLIP RIVER RESERVES
No Clasps Issued
Roll No. 39

Chief Leader	MEYER L.W.
Leader	NIENABER B.J.
	RAUTENBACH G.H.
Sub-Leader	BREBNER J.H.
	CHANDLER W.H.
Sgt.	D'ARCY J.H.
	FARRELL J.R.
	ZIETSMAN H.J.
Cpl.	COLLING F.
	DEWAAL P.J.
	MARITZ A.A.
	MELLIS J.H.
	POTGIETER L.J.
	POTGIETER M.H.

Cpl. VAN REENEN G.F.
ZIETSMAN W.J.
Tpr. ADAMS C.
ALBERTS N.J.
BOERS A.G.J.
BOOTH S.S.
BLOY D.F.
BYLOO J.P.
COETZER W.J.G.
COVENTRY H.
COVENTRY V.E.
DAVIS J.
DE JONGH C.
FARQUHAR J.A.
FARRELL J.T.
FUHRIE L.P.
HATTIAGH I.J.
HATTIAGH W.A.
HAWORTH E.J.
HYDE H.O.
JONES J.D
LELLO H.E.
LE ROUX G.
LOMBARD J.J.
MANN W.H.
MARAIS B.G.
MARAIS C.F.
MOORE G.
NEL C.J.
NEL J.C.
NEL P.R.
NIENABER B.J. (Jnr)
PORTSMOUTH W.
POTGIETER D.F.
POTGIETER F.P.
POTGEITER G.
POTGEITER J.P.
POTGIETER L.J.
POTGIETER M.J.
PRETORIUS J.A.
PRICE J.
SMITH V.H.
SNYMAN P.M.B.
SPICER H.W.
THORROLD G.
UMPLEBY G.
VAN DER LEEUW K.J.
WHITHAM B.

Total of 62 Awards

With Clasps - Nil

No Clasps - 62

KRANTZKOP RESERVES
With Clasp 1906
Roll No. 47

Chief Leader VAN ROOYEN F.E.
Leader DE WAAL J.A.
VAN ROOYEN H.L.
VERMAAK P.R.
Sub-Leader PROKSCH L.L.
VAN ROOYEN T.J.
QMS SHAKELTON T.J.
Sgt. NEL P.J.
VAN ROOYEN C.J.
VAN ROOYEN J.C.
Sgt. VAN ROOYEN L.J.N.
Cpl. AMBLER A.W.
HAVEMANN L.M.J.
JOHNSON L.P.
KOCH H.G.
NEL P.J.
VAN ROOYEN G.H.
VAN ROOYEN J.H.
Tpr. BOAST W.R.
BOMFORD G.H.
CLARENCE L.W.
DALE G.
FRASER G.H.
GREENHALGH N.W.
HAVEMAN A.G.
HERBERT T.
IRWIN J.
KIRKMAN S.E.
KOCH H.A.
KOCH H.W.
LANDSBERG C.H.
LANDSBERG D.J.
MARTENS D.J.
MARTENS J.C.
MARTENS (D.J. Son) J.T.
MARTENS (J.T. Son) J.T.
MARTENS R.P.
MORGAN H.
NEL G.
NEL J.P.
NEL J.S.
NEL J.S.L.
NEL L.J.
NEL L.J.
NEL L.L.
NEL L.M.J.
NUSS F.H.
PAGE H.A.
PERRY C.J.
POTGIETER L.J.
REIBLING W.
SOHLIN A.
VAN NIEKERK J.A.
VAN ROOYEN C.J.
VAN ROOYEN G.H.
VAN ROOYEN G.H.C.
VAN ROOYEN H.L.
VAN ROOYEN H.P.
VAN ROOYEN I.M.
VAN ROOYEN J.P.
VAN ROOYEN L.M.
VAN ROOYEN L.N.J.
VAN ROOYEN L.M.J.
VAN ROOYEN P.J.N.
VAN ROOYEN T.J.
VAN ROOYEN W.M.J.
VAN ROOYEN W.M.J.
VAN ROOYEN W.W.
WILSON H.E.
ZIETSMAN C.J.
ZIETSMAN G.P.

No Clasps Issued

Cpl. LAMB F.T.
Tpr. KEYTER J.
MARTENS J.C.
SMITH R.N.

Total of 75 Awards

With Clasps - 71
No Clasps - 4

LANCASHIRE & YORKSHIRE CONTINGENT
With Clasp 1906
Roll No. 7

Lt.Col.	PEAKMAN T.C.
Capt/Adj.	HELBERT G.G.H.
Lt.	ANDERSON R.
	CURRIE C.G.I.
	HAIR R.K.
	JENNISON H.
	LOWDEN H.E.
Sgt/Maj.	FORBES W.J.
QMS	STEEL W.E.
Sgt.	HALE J.
	JONES F.O.
	REDFEARN H.L.
	SOPPITT H.A.P.
	TETLEY J.F.
Cpl.	BARNES J.W.
	BOTHWELL S.
	HOWELL C.W.
	LANGDON S.
	LAZARUS J.
	MACKAY J.G.
	THOMAS E.A.
	WARDELL A.J.
	WILLIAMS R.E.
	YOUNG W.
Tpr.	AITKEN J.
	BETTINGTON R.O.
	BRADFORD J.
	CASE R.V.
	COLLIER E.N.
	FORD A.E.
	GILLIES M.
	GREGORY J.N.
	GRIFFIN W.B.
	HARRINGTON D.
	HUNTER J.B.
	JOHNSON F.W.
	KING C.
	LAWLOR J.T.
	LUMGAIR D.
	McDONALD A.
	McDONALD T.P.
	MUNRO F.
	MURGATROYD J.
	MURGATROYD T.A.
	ROBERTS T.
	SHAW H.
Pte.	ALLEN H.
	ANDREWS B.
	BEER S.
	BELL G.
	BERRY C.T.
	BERRY T.I.
	BIBBY W.P.
	BIRCH G.B.
	BLACKBURN C.
	BRECKELL T.R.
	BROWNE W.H.
	CHRYSTAL J.
	CLARK W.H.C.
	CLARKE E.P.
	CLARKSON W.P.
	COKE G.I.
	CONE T.
	COTTER J.W.
	COWGILL F.W.
	CRAWFORD A.H.
	CREAMER S.
	DAHL T.O.
	DANIELS T.
Pte.	DAW E.M.
	DENNY W.G.
	DOHERTY G.
	DOHERTY T.
	DUTFIELD H.
	EDMUNDSON J.
	ELLIOTT G.
	FARRICKER J.E.
	FAY J.
	FILTNESS D.
	FITZMAURICE J.
	GILLISPIER.
	HALL D.
	HARDY P.
	HARRHY J.
	HARPER A.
	HART B.
	HARTLEY E.J.
	HAWKINS J.
	HAYTHORNTHWAITE G.
	HEATON I.
	HILL S.
	HOLLINGWORTH J.
	HORN H.
	HUBAND W.
	HUMPHREYS C.
	JEFFERSON A.
	JOHNSTON V.J.
	JONES F.E.
	JONES H.J.S.
	JORDAN A.
	KEYS E.F.
	KEYS R.G.
	KING T.
	KINNAIRD J.A.
	LAMBERT J.H.
	LEAVESLEY J.
	LENG W.
	LITTLEWOOD T.J.
	LOCK J.A.
	LOCKWOOD A.S.
	LOCKWOOD E.G.
	LOWE C.
	LYNCH J.
	MARCHANT J.
	McDOWELL D.
	McKENZIE H.
	MORONEY J.
	MORRISON F.C.
	MUIR T.
	NEALE A.B.
	PALK A.G.
	PATTER W.
	POOLE L.R.
	PRICE M.
	PROUD J.
	RABBITTS W.H.
	READ W.
	REEESE C.G.
	ROBERTS J.W.
	RODERICK T.
	SCOLLARD N.
	SIMCOCK J.H.
	SINCLAIR J.
	SKEVINGTON W.H.
	TAYLOR C.
	TAYLOR F.
	THESEN H.O.
	THOMAS P.A.
	TODD J.
	TULLY A.
	WALKER R.H.
	WATSON J.

Pte.	WATSON J.H.
	WATT G.
	WHITE C.E.
	WHITWANE T.W.
	WILLIAMS W.H.
	WILSON P.
	WRIGHT H.
	WYER E.E.

Total of 150 Awards

With Clasps - 150

No Clasps - Nil

LOWER TUGELA RESERVES
No Clasps Issued
Roll No. 58

Sub-Leader	HULETT A.S.L.
Revd.	COOMBE E.W.
Sgt.	GREENLY A.P.
	HOPKINS E.A.
Cpl.	HULETT W.A.
	MILLICAN J.J.
Tpr.	ANDERSON T.
	BALCOMB B.
	BALCOMB F.
	BALCOMB H.
	BALCOMB I.
	BALCOMB L.
	BALCOMB O.
	BINNIE J.
	BOURNE E.H.
	BRANDON N.J.
	BULL E.
	BULL H.
	ELLIS W.J.
	EMERSON H.L.
	FIDDES G.S.
	HINDSON E.
	HINDSON R.
	HINDSON W.R.
	HULETT E.F.W.
	HULETT H.B.
	HULETT J.B.
	MILLICAN T.
	NEILSEN N.
	NIGHTINGALE L.R.
	OLSEN O.
	PEARSON J.V.
	PIETERS B.H.
	RORVIK S.
	STONES J.P.

Total of 35 Awards

With Clasps - Nil

No Clasps - 35

MEIMOTH RESERVES
With Clasp 1906
Roll No. 57

Chief Leader	WHITE F.W.
Leader	PRETORIUS A.L.
Q/M	DIXON J.N.R.
S/Maj.	BASSAGE J.
Sgt.	KRUGER E.H.C.
QMS	CHENNELL B.
Cpl.	LIVERSAGE G.
	SMITH T.W.F.
Pte.	BARNARD J.J.
	BOND F.
	BOSMAN J.
	DELPORT A.
	DORFLING F.
	DU PREEZ D.
	DU PREEZ J.
	FERREIRA S.P.
	MAXWELL H.M.
	McGENEGAL F.S.
	MOOLMAN C.
	MOOLMAN J.P.
	PRETORIUS D.J. (Jnr)
	SMITH F.
	SMITH T.W.F.
	STRYDOM W.
	WINFIELD M.H.

No Clasps Issued

Leader	RANDELHOFF W.E.
	SYMMONDS A.W.
QMS	DE HAAS D.
Sgt.	MACKESON A.
Cpl.	HUNSLEY C.
Pte.	ACKERMANN J.
	BAILEY S.
	BANNISTER T.W.
	BLANCHE J.C.L.
	BRONKHORST J.J.
	BRONKHORST R.J.
	BRONKHORST S.J.
	DAY A.E.
	FERREIRA J.M.
	LEE W.
	LIVERSAGE E.A.
	MARITZ S.
	McPARLIN E.O.
	MOOLMAN J.
	ORTLEPP W.G.
	POTGIETER J. (Jnr)
	PRETORIUS D.J.
	PRETORIUS D.J. (Jnr)
	SMITH T.A.
	STRYDOM F.J.
	TAIT S.J.
	TEMPLETON R.
	VAN ROOYEN C.J.
	VAN ROOYEN C.P.
	VAN ROOYEN J.J.
	VERMAAK H.G.
	WILSON F.D.

Total of 57 Awards

With Clasps - 25

No Clasps - 32

MILITIA RESERVES LOWER TUGELA DIVISION
No Clasps Issued
Roll No. 34

Leader	CLARK H.A.
	JACKSON A.E.
	ROBBINS W.C.

Sub-Leader	HAKWINS E.	Conduct.	MANN W.H.
QMS	BAYER W.J.		MAY A.L.
Sgt.	BOND A.T.		McKENZIE J.
	IVINS J.H.		MENEELY H.
Cpl.	FLETCHER G.		NEL J.H.
	PAIGE H.G.		PERRY M.F.
	SMITH H.C.		POALSES E.
	WEBB F.C.		RICHTER D.
	WOOLRIDGE W.H.		VAN DER WESTHUYZEN J.
Pte.	BRUCE W.P.		WARREN W.M.
	DAHL A.E.		WEBSTER B.A.
	FORBEY F.		WILLIAMS D.
	FORD S.T.	Sgt.	CAMPBELL R.
	FREEMAN J.		COLLINS R.W.T.
	FREUIN G.		CROSS W.H.
	FULLER H.		FOOTE A.W.
	GIELINK E.		HOLMES F.J.B.
	GIELINK W.		HOWE F.O.L.
	GOSLING J.		TAYLOR W.S.
	GRAHAM W.S.		WORMINGTON C.
	GRAYSON C.	Driver	ADAMS C.
	HALL T.H.		ALLBRECHT A.
	HANSEN A.		BLOEM W.
	HOKAN J.		DAVIS JIM
	JENNER J.		DAVIS JOHN
	JOHNSON T.		FISHER C.
	JOHNSON W.		LUCASI M.
	KIRBY T.H.		NATCHEY S.
	KOSTER G.		NELSON D.
	LINES C.T.		RUITER J.
	MARSE J.		RYLAND P.
	REUTERINK A.		VAN WYK J.
	REUTERINK J.		VESAZIE F.
	ROCKLIFF R.A.		WILLIAMS J.
	RODE C.		WRIGHT J.
	RODE H.		
	SCHEFFER J.	No Clasps Issued	
	SCHEFFER W.		
	SHUTTER F.P.	Conduct.	ABRAHAMS A.
	SMITHERS W.H.		ADAMS J.D.
	SUMMERS W.R.W.		ATHERSTONE H.M.
	SUTCLIFF R.B.		BARNARD J.
	THEISSEN T.		CRAWFORD A.
	THRING D.		DARFEL J.
	VAN DER HOVEN R.W.		ENGELBRECHT J.M.
	VAN DER WAGEN W.		FORD F.
	VENTON G.H.		GREEN F.D.
	WARRY F.		GREEN H.H.
	WEBB J.		HIGGS G.W.
			McKENZIE E.J.D.
			SHACKLEFORD W.J.
			WEARNE W.S.
		Sgt.	GREGORY T.
			KNOLLYS F.R.
		Driver	ADAMS F.
			BUSSON J.
			DAVIDS M.
			ELLS G.J.
			FOUNTAIN A.
			HARVEY A.
			JACKSON E.
			MANTO R.
			MGATI T.
			PEMBLETON J.
			RAATZ J.
			VAN ROOYAN J.

Total of 52 Awards

With Clasps - Nil

No Clasps - 52

MILITIA TRANSPORT SERVICE CORPS.
With Clasp 1906
Roll No. 10

Lt.	ADAMS A.T.
	MARKHAM B.T.K.
S/Maj.	KNAPP C.D.
Conduct.	ALLWRIGHT W.H.
	BIRD C.D.
	BULLEN A.
	CHURCHILL G.
	COOPER D.G.
	COOPER W.E.
	COOTE W.

Total of 73 Awards

With Clasps - 45

No Clasps - 28

NATAL CARBINEERS
With Clasp 1906
Roll No. 15

Col.	McKENZIE D. KCB CB KMG VD
Lt.Col.	CROMPTON B.
	MACKAY D.W.
	RODWELL
	SHEPSTONE W.S.
	WEIGHTON J.
Major	COMRIE W.
	GAGE W.T.
	OWEN T.M.
	SMALLIE A.W.
	TOWNSEND A.C.
Captain	ALLISON T.J.
	BARTER E.W.
	BRANDON R.A.L.
	BRISCOE J.E.
	COCKBURN R.A.
	GRAY W.P.
	MONTGOMERY J.W.V.
	RICHARDS G.R.
	SMITH R.W.
	TANNER R.M.
Lt.QM	McKENZIE J.
	RICHMOND R.A.
Lt.	ANTEL W.E.
	BAXTER E.W.
	BEATTY K.J.
	BLACK W.
	BLAKER G.E.
	COPE C.F.J.
	DICKINSON P.G.
	FANNIN J.G.
	HAMPSON B.A.
	HOME W.H.
	JOHNSON J.W.
	KEMP C.G.
	LANGLEY A.S.
	LINDSAY R.W.
	MARTIN B.W.
	MERRICK S.R.
	PATERSON C.M.
	RYLEY H.
	SMITH J.H.
	SMYTHE J.O.
	STIEBEL F.H.
	STRIDE P.W.
	THORNHILL H.C.
	TODD A.E.
	VANDERPLANK A.B.
	WALSH J.D.
	WALTON D.
	WALTON H.
RSM	BURKIMSHER W.
S/Major	HIGGINS P.J.
Bandmast.	KIELLY J.
SSM	ANDERSON G.C.
	McCATHIE T.
	MEYER J.H.
	MITCHELL T.
	PANNEWITZ A.J.
	PATON D.
	STEVENS W.P.
	SWAN A.
	WILKINSON H.
QMS	CASTLE T.A.
	HARKER G.
	SANDERS W.H.
	THOMPSON D.
Farr.QMS	SANDEMAN W.
	WALSH A.H.
SQMS	CARTER C.R.
	DUNN D.J.
	HARTE W.H.P.
	KEAN E.J.
	MORELAND H.H.S.
	NEWTON T.
	OSBORN W.J.
	RAPSON H.E.
	RAW R.J.
	SHAW W.L.
SIM	ZUNCKEL E.C.
OR/Sgt.	KRUGER A.H.O.
	WATTS R.
Staff Sgt.	CAMPBELL C.H.
Sgt.Farr.	BINGHAM F.E.
	HALL J.
	NICHOLSON J.
	PROCTOR A.H.
	QUESTED W.E.
Sgt.Sadler	LYLE T.J.
	ROGERS J.
Sgt.Tailor	WALTERS W.H. DCM
Sgt. Trumpt.	CRAIG H.A.
	FAIRALL G.W.
Sgt.	BENNETT G.F.
	BOYD F.W.
	BUNTTING B.B.
	BUTTON C.E.R.
	CAMPBELL E.W.
	COOKE H.
	CRAGG T.R.
	CRAW A.P.
	DICKS E.I. MSM
	DICKS G.W.
	DICKS J.
	DICKINSON A.B.
	FARMER F.C.
	GRAHAM J.J.
	GRANT A.F.
	GRANT W.H.
	HALL W.A.
	HARDING E.A.C.
	HATHORN F.H.
	HATHORN H.
	HATLEY C.
	HAYES E.H.
	HOUSEHOLD E.E.
	HUMPHRIES J.
	JOYCE B.W.
	KENNEDY C.
	LANGLEY C.H.
	LITTLE T.D.
	LYALL A.
	MADSEN A.
	MADSEN M.
	MASON A.J.
	McLEAN H.
	MEARES H.
	MELLIS G.H.
	MITCHELL W.H.
	MITCHELL W.J.
	MORELAND E.B.
	MULCAHY C.L.H.
	NEWLANDS G.
	PETERS J.
	PHILLIPS G.
	PHIPSON H.C.

Sgt.	POTTOW B.C.T.	Cpl.	RENNIE J.
	ROBINSON T.J.		RILEY J.
	SCLANDERS D.G.		ROBINSON F.C.
	SHAW H.N.		SAVAGE S.
	STEVENS G.Y.		SHUTTLEWORTH W.H.
	SUTHERLAND J.		SKOTTOWE C.R.
	SYMES W.		SMITHWICK P.F.
	TALBOT B.D.		STEAD B.L.
	TALBOT W.A.		STEAD H.P.
	TEASDALE H.		STEVENS B.J.
	THOMSON G.L.		STEVENS F.N.
	TOPHAM F.J.C.		STIRTON C.H.
	URQUHART H.J.		STRANACK W.G.
	WARWICK T.E.		THRASH C.E.H.
	WILES H.W.		TODD E.C.
	WRAY B.		URQUHART J.P.
	WRIGHT W.E.		WALKER J.H.
L/Sgt.	PRATT H.		WALLBRIDGE A.C.
Cpl.SS	DERRICK J.		WARWICK P.D.
	NELSON E.N.		WHITE W.W.
Cpl.Trumpt.			YUNNIE J.L.
	GIREAUDEAU R.H.	L/Cpl.	CHRISTOPHER V.J.M.
	ROWLES E.O.		DICKS A.F.
Cpl.	ANDERSON J.M.		HACKLAND T.
	ANTEL R.J.M.		HOLCOMB W.G.
	BENNETT E.F.L.		HOLDING C.W.
	BISSETT J.J.		HOUSEHOLD T.H.
	BLAKE A.V.E.		KING W.W.
	BUCHANAN A.D.		LAMBLE F.
	BURNS J.		LINDSAY J.R.
	BUACH W.M.		MACPHAIL D.D.
	CAMPBELL A.J.E.		McLEAN W.
	CAMPBELL H.A.		OTTO C.S.D.
	CARTER A.		RANDLES R.T.
	CATCHPOLE H.J.		ROSS A.
	CHATER A.B.		SAMUELSON S.V.
	COMRIE J.M.		SYMES T.
	CRATHORNE B.		VAN DER MERWE W.P.
	CROUCH W.J.	Tmptr.	ARMSTRONG E.G.
	CULVERWELL C.		HARBURN C.D.
	DICKS H.C.		RITTER E.A.
	DICKS H.E.H.	Tpr.	ABBOT E.
	DICKS J.A.		ADAMS A.E.
	ELLISON G.		ADDIS S.R.
	ELY H.G.		ADDISON D.
	FARMER J.E.		ADDISON V.
	FRIDAY L.		AHRENS F.W.
	GAGE W.J.		ALBERS H.F.
	GRANT N.J.		ALDIR H.G.
	GREIG J.E.		ANDERSON A.
	HAIR J.		ANDERSON C.E.
	HARDING J.J.		ANDERSON D.
	HATLEY H.W.		ANDERSON G.
	JACKSON C.D.		ANDERSON J.
	JACKSON T.A.		ANDERSON P.
	JACKSON W.		ANDREWS G.F.
	KENDALL J.W.		ANDREWS R.G.H.
	KING C.J.R.		ANGUS J.
	KING F.E.		ANLEY F.G.
	KING L.J.		ANTEL H.J.
	KREMER G.F.		ANTHONY A.
	LAVERTON J.		ARBUCKLE E.D.
	LAYMAN C.F.		ARBUCKLE R.O.
	McCULLOUGH J.		ARBUTHNOT O.C.
	McCULLOUGH W.		ARCHER G.H.F.
	McKENZIE N.		ARNOLD R.G.
	McKENZIE R.		ASH A.G.
	MEYER F.		ASHBY L.F.
	MEYER H.F.		ASHBY W.
	MILLER G.D.S.		ATKINSON W.B.
	MITCHELL H.T.		AYRTON F.S.
	NICHOLSON J.B.		BAIKIE I.M.
	PRAETORIOUS A.		BAILEY W.

Tpr.	BALL B.A.	Tpr.	COATES J.
	BALL S.		COCKCROFT G.P.
	BALLENTYNE P.		COCKCROFT H.G.
	BAMBER C.W.		COCKROFT D.A.W.
	BARFIELD G.		COLLINS C.
	BARKER J.S.		COLLINS E.F.
	BARKER W.E.		COLLIS S.F.
	BARNETT C.		COLQUHOUN F.W.
	BARTHOLOMEW P.J.		COLLYER G.
	BAWDEN J.F.		COLLYER H.
	BAWDEN W.P.		COLLYER J.
	BAXTER W.S.		COLVILLE C.
	BEATTIE R.G.		COLVILLE G.K.
	BEDDOWS T.A.		COOKE J.
	BEHR P.		COOPER F.R.
	BELL B.		CORDINER W.
	BESTER I.J.		CORNFORTH E.
	BESTER T.C.		COVENTRY A.T.
	BIGGS R.F.		COVENTRY H.N.
	BISHOP R.E.		CRAIG W.
	BLACKLER C.		CRAWLEY F.H.
	BLYTON P.G.		CROSSLEY F.
	BOURK W.E.		CULLINGWORTH A.W.
	BOWMAN H.D.K.		CULVERWELL C.W.
	BOYCE W.S.		CULVERWELL R.
	BOYD N.		CULVERWELL R.H.
	BOYER F.H.		CUNDILL G.T.
	BRAADVEDT J.		DANIEL E.J.
	BRANDON F.J.T.		DANIELS J.W.
	BRAZIER M.		DAUBER J.B.
	BRISTO J.		DAVIDSON A.
	BROADBENT H.S.		DAVIDSON F.E.F.
	BROMLEY E.		DAVIDSON W.E.G.
	BROWN C.W.		DAVIES J.H.
	BROWN D.J.		DAVIS F.
	BROWN F.J.		DE BARY F.P.H.
	BROWN H.		DE HAAS J.E.P.
	BROWN G.L.		DE JAAGER L.P.
	BROWN J.		DE LA HUNT A.H.
	BROWN J.G.		DENTON F.
	BRYAN C.P.		DESPARD H.O.B.
	BUCHANAN A.M.		DE VALANCE G.
	BUNTING D.		DE WAAL P.J.
	BUNTTING G.F.		DEWAR W.R.
	BURFORD R.		DICKS C.G.
	BURNARD F.B.		DICKS C.G.
	BURNS G.		DICKS R.I.
	BURNS P.		DIMOCK G.A.G.
	BUSH A.H.		DINKELMAN A.H.
	BUTCHER F.J.		DIX A.E.
	BUTLER M.		DOLAN T.
	BUXTON W.		DONALD A.
	CAIRNIE A.		DOUGLAS C.
	CAIRNS A.K.		DREW H.G.
	CAIRNS J.K.		DRIVER E.F.
	CAMERON C.		DRUMMOND W.
	CAMERON W.		DU BOIS E.O.
	CAMPBELL D.R.		DUFF J.
	CAMPBELL J.A.		DURHAM J.
	CAMPBELL R.B.		DYMES H.F.V.
	CANDLER F.J.		EARL T.G.
	CATCHPOLE A.H.		ECCLES H.B.
	CATCHPOLE T.P. MSM		ECCLES V.J.L.
	CAWOOD I.B.		EDGAR E.
	CHAMBERS P.G.		EDMONDS G.O.
	CHENALLS J.		EDMONDS H.C.
	CHENEY B.A.		EVANS D.B.
	CHRISTIE L.M.		EWEN W.
	CHURCHILL J.H.		FAIRALL W.C.
	CLARENCE L.R.		FAIRHEAD J.T.
	CLARENCE V.B.		FAYERS W.M.
	CLARENCE W.N.		FITZWILLIAM C.
	CLENDENNEN A.		FORD E.W.

Tpr.	FORDER C.E.	Tpr.	HODDER J.
	FORSYTH W.H.		HODGSON H.E.
	FOSTER M.		HOGBEN E.E.
	FOWLER R.R.		HOLE W.H.
	FOX W.G.		HOLLARD W.E.
	FRANCIS B.		HOLMES G.W.G.
	FRANCIS J.W.		HOLMES J.W.
	FRANKISH F.H.		HOOD E.H.
	FYRTH J.		HORNBY H.M.
	GALLAGHER M.J.		HORSBURGH J.
	GARBETT H.E.		HOUSEHOLD F.P.
	GARDNER P.L.		HOWARD W.
	GASS E.A.		HOWIE W.
	GEBERS W.F.		HUGHES H.R.
	GEDDES S.J.		HUMBERSTONE R.
	GEILS A.W.		IMBER A.
	GEORGE E.		ISAACS G.A.
	GIBSON J.		JACKSON A.
	GIFFORD F.A.		JACOBS L.M.
	GILBERT C.F.		JAFFRAY J.B.
	GILBERT J.E.		JAMESON A.
	GILLAM R.H.		JARVIS C.W.
	GOODWILL H.P.		JOHNSON A.L.
	GORDON J.K.		JOHNSON C.M.
	GORDON R.E.		JOHNSON E.E.
	GRANT F.H.		JOHNSTON J. (1082)
	GRANT J.		JOHNSTON J. (5190)
	GRAVERS W.		JOHNSTONE A.E.
	GRAY G.W.		JOHNSTONE B.
	GRAY H.E.		JOHNSTONE J.
	GREEN C.G.		JONES F.D.
	GREENE G.E.		JONES F. ST. G.
	GRIFFIN W.B.		JONES F.T.
	GROOM E.A.		JONES H.A.
	GROOM F.E.		JONES J.H.
	GROOM T.R.		JONES R.
	GUTHRIE J.		JONES R.A.
	GUTTERSON G.		JONES S.N.
	GUY P.		JONES W.P.
	HACKLAND H.C.		KEEL W.A.
	HACKLAND R.B.		KEEL W.J.
	HAGGERTY H.		KEIGHTLEY W.G.J.
	HAILSTONE W.S.		KELLY A.D.
	HAIR A.J.		KELLY A.E.
	HALL A.A.		KEYES M.W.
	HALL H.B.		KILGOUR P.
	HAMILTON W.G.		KING E.
	HAMMIL M.		KING J.R.
	HAMPSON G.R.		KIRBY V.A.
	HARBURN T.A.		KNAPP W.F.
	HARDING E.C.J.		LADD W.
	HARDMAN C.E.		LADDS C.G.
	HARKER W.M.		LANG B.M.
	HARRIL F.P.		LANG R.A.
	HATHORN A.A.R.		LANG T.
	HATLEY F.N.		LARSEN J.O.
	HAW C.		LARSEN M.
	HAWORTH A.C.		LATIMER E.J.
	HAWTON R.W.		LAW A.
	HAYES C.E.		LAWRENCE T.W.
	HAZELFOOT C.R.W.		LAWSON R.
	HEARN R.J.R.		LEATHERN G.
	HECKLER F.G.		LEATHERN W.
	HECKLER J.A.		LEHMANN W.W.
	HENDRY A.R.		LEMMON A.
	HENDRY H.J.		LIMOUZIN G.A.
	HENWOOD N.N.		LINDSAY A.M.
	HEURTLEY C.T.		LINDSAY F.S.
	HEWITT F.R.		LINDSAY H.R.
	HILL H.		LINDSAY J.A.V.
	HILL N.		LISHMAN G.
	HILL W.J.		LLOYD H.C.
	HISCOCK H.		LLOYD R.

Tpr.	LOCKE J.	Tpr.	MORTIMER T.A.
	LOGAN R.O.		MORTON J.W.
	LONG C.E.		MOSS E.
	LOVE J.		MUIRHEAD A.
	LOWE C.F.		MUIRHEAD O.J.M.
	LOWE D.A.		MULCAHY H.F.H.
	LUCKINS L.W.		MULLIGAN J.
	LUGG C.E.		MUNRO A.G.
	MacDONALD R.		MURPHY J.
	MACK A.L.		MURRAY J.
	MACK C.C.		MURRAY J.H.
	MACK E.S.		MUSSON F.T.
	MacNAUGHTON A.		NADONALD J.E.
	MacPHERSON W.		NEIZEL W.A.
	MacQUEEN G.		NEL H.N.
	MALCOLM E.W.		NEL O.R.
	MALCOLM G.		NELSON P.C.
	MALCOLM R.D.		NEVILL P.G.
	MARKS E.P.		NORRIS H.
	MARSH W.S.		NURSE A.J.
	MASON P.A.		NURSE E.J.
	MASON P.R.		O'BRIEN J.M.
	MASON S.N.		O'BRIEN R.W.H.
	MASON W.V. (1271)		ORLEANS Prince A of:-
	MASON W.V. (1468)		OSBORNE H.D.
	MASSON T.		OTTO R.V.
	MATTHEW A.		OVER J.E.
	MATTHEW A.E.		OXLAND L.O.
	MATTHEWS G.E.		PARKS T.W.
	MATTHEWS R,T,		PAYNE H.W.
	McCULLOUGH A.L.		PEARSON A.
	McCULLOUGH W.A.		PEARSON A.M.
	McDONALD H.H.		PEEL A.E.
	McDONALD J.		PENNELLS F.J.
	McDONALD R.		PETTIGREW J.M.B.
	McFEETERS H.		PHIPSON H.A.
	McFIE J.T.		PHIPSON K.A.
	McKENZIE J.H.		PHIPSON L.L.
	McKENZIE K.A.		PHIPSON S.C.
	McKENZIE K.R.		PIETERSE B.J.
	McKNIGHT J.		PIETERSE F.J. (1386)
	McLEAN W.J.B.		PIETERSE F.J. (1387)
	McLEOD A.M.		PIETERSE F.J. (1388)
	McLEOD F.		PIETERSE F.J. (1577)
	McMULLEN G.S.		PIETERSE J.C.
	McPHERSON N.		PIETERSE S.
	McWILLIAM J.		PIM J.W.
	McWILLIAM T.		PITMAN C.A.
	McWILLIAMS W.		POLE A.G.J.
	METHLEY H.F.		POOK L.J.
	MEYER A.		POOLE S.A.
	MEYER G.C.		POOLEY H.
	MEYER J.E.		POTTOW C.R.
	MILES J.L.B.		POTTOW J.U.A.
	MILLER A.		PRETORIOUS J.H.
	MILLER J.H.		PRICHARD L.J.
	MILLER W.S.J.		RALFE J.
	MILLS A.J.		RANDLES W.
	MILNE J.V.		RATHBONE E.
	MITCHELL J.N.		RATHBONE G.E.
	MITCHELL W.		RATHBONE H.A.
	MOGGRIDGE J.W.A.		RATHBONE T.
	MOLLER H.C.		RATSEY A.E.
	MOLLER M.C.		RAVERTY L.
	MONTGOMERY Q.H.		RAW K.P.
	MORAN C.C.		RAW L.C.
	MORCOM H.B.		RAW R.
	MORELAND G.H.		RAWLINSON F.C.
	MORELAND J.M.		RAWNSLEY T.M.
	MORRIS J.F.		REDMAN G.
	MORRIS J.H.		REDMAN J.
	MORRISON T.H.		REED J.
	MORROW G.		REID J.W.

Tpr.	REID T.H.	Tpr.	STEVENS C.H.
	RICHARDS W.H.		STEVENS F.
	RICHARDSON M.		STEWART H.A.
	RILEY T.		STEWART J.
	RILEY W.		STEWART J.R.
	RIVERS R.C.		STICKLES C.
	RIX G.E.		STILWELL C.R.
	ROBBIE A.B.		STOCKIL E.C.
	ROBBINS B.		STOCKIL F.
	ROBDE E.		STOCKIL J.C.
	ROBERTSON A.J.		STONE R.M.
	ROBERTSON J.W.		STONE W.G.
	ROBINS W.H.		STRACHAN A.G.
	ROBINSON A.H.		STRAWSON W.B.
	ROBINSON E.E.		STUART A.W.
	ROBINSON P.		STUART W.A.
	ROBINSON W.W.		SURGEON T.
	ROBSON F.W.J.		SWAN A.L.
	ROGERS W.		SWART J.
	ROSS A.C.		SWINDON C.M.
	ROSS A.G.		SWINDON H.G.
	ROSS A.W.		SYMONS P.M.
	ROSS D.M.		SYMONS R.E.
	ROSS J.		TATHAM H.C.
	RUMPF F.		TAYLOR A.E.
	RUTHERFORD P.B.		TAYLOR G.L.
	RUTHERFORD R.H.		TAYLOR H.A.
	SALTER A.W.		TAYLOR L.W.
	SAMUELSON R.O.		TAYLOR W.T.
	SCHAFER A.W.		TENNENT L.C.
	SCHALKWYK J.S.		THOMPSON A.C.
	SCHIFFER C.C.		THOMPSON W.
	SCHUMAN F.T.		THOMPSON W.C.
	SCHWEGMANN A.W.R.		THORBURN W.
	SCLATER W.J.		THORNHILL C.C.
	SCOTT F.M.		THORNE W.
	SEAGER A.		TODD H.B.
	SEAGER H.F.		TOMLINSON L.W.
	SEAGER H.W.		TOMLINSON R.
	SERRIDGE H.		TOSH J.
	SEWARD A.J.		TRAFFORD W.F.
	SHARP J.K.		TRAVERS H.
	SHAW F.W.		TREMEARNE P.H.
	SHEPHERD W.		TRODD R.
	SHORES A.T.		TROTTER J.E.N.
	SHUM N.W.		TURNLEY H.E.
	SIDDAL A.J.		TUTHILL W.
	SIM E.S.		TWITE A.L.
	SIME E.E.		VALENTINE R.
	SIMMONS L.H.		VAN AART J.W.
	SIMPSON R.O.		VANDERLEUR J.C.
	SIMPSON S.		VAN DER MERWE J.L.
	SINCLAIR W.		VARTY A.E.
	SKOTTOWE C.M.B.		VARTY C.B.
	SKOTTOWE J.A.		VEAR W.
	SKOTTOWE J.B.		WADE E.
	SLATTERY A.E.		WADE G.H.
	SMITH D.G.		WADE J.B.
	SMITH H.P.		WALES C.D.
	SMITH M.		WALKER H.P.
	SONLEY J.W.		WALSH J.G.
	SPENCER C.R.		WALSH W.
	SPIERS F.W.		WAUGH C.R.
	SPRINGORUM A.F.W.		WHEELER A.E.
	SPROSON J.F.		WHEELER C.
	SPURR F.		WHITE R.
	STABLEFORD H.V.		WHYSALL C.W.
	STACEY F.		WHYSALL H.
	ST. AUSTIN E.R.M.		WILLIAMS C.
	STANLEY J.		WILLIAMS G.S.
	STANSFIELD H.W.		WILLIAMS W.D.

Tpr.	WILKINSON D.E.	Tpr.	GRANT V.J.
	WILKINSON W.G.		GREENE C.M.
	WINSOR W.S.		GREEN W.H.
	WISENER P.		HALLET H.E.
	WOOD E.R.		HARDMAN R.C.
	WOOD J.		HARDY W.J.
	WOODHOUSE W.F.		HARRIS R.
	WOODINGTON D.S.M.		HENRY D.A.
	WOODS E.A.		HOBBS J.F.
	WOODS T.E.		HOGAN J.M.
	WOODS V.J.		HORSHAM J.S.
	WRIGHT A.		HUGHES S.E.
	WYNNE T..		HULLEY F.W.
	ZUNCKEL A.O.		HULLEY H.C.
	ZUNCKEL O.S.L.		HULLEY R.W.
	ZUNCKEL T.C.		HUNT J.V.
			IRWIN R.S.
No Clasps Issued			JAMES C.H.
			JERRAM R.
Lt.Col.	HAIR A.		JOHNSON J.
SSM	BRYAN H.		KELLY F.W.
	SULLIVAN E.		KIRSCHBERG M.H.
SQMS	BENNETT M.W.		LALLY J.A.
Sgt.Farr.	HARRISON S.		LAWRENCE A.R.
Sgt.	BUTTER F.G.		LEDEBOER C.M.
	KELLY M.		LINDSAY W.H.
Cpl.	COOKE H.H.		LINDUP R.
	EDGINTON A.E.		LLOYD A.R.S.
	FISH E.		LOBBAN G.
	FULLER W.R.		MACURDY A.
	HENWOOD H.H.		MANN P.L.
	LANG W.A.		McDERMOT J.
L/Cpl.	RANSOM F.J.		McKENZIE L.G.
Tpr.	AITKEN A.B.		McKILLOP D.
	ANDERSON E.A.		MERCER H.R.
	ANDERSON G.		MERCER W.J.
	ANDREWS H.A.J.		MILLER A. (5237)
	ARCHIBALD W.R.		MORTON J.H.
	ASHTON T.B.		MULLER J.
	BAKER A.J.		NASH P.
	BEGG A.A.		NEEDHAM G.
	BELL F.H.		NEVILLE P.S.
	BRENCHLEY J.		NORTON G.H.
	BULKLEY J.P.		OWEN A.J.
	BULLOUGH A.		PATERSON A.
	BURGESS N.L.		POWYS R.
	BURMAN M.J.		PRATT E.E.
	BURROWS M.		PRATT O.H.
	BURN A.		RETTER A.
	BUTLER M.		RICHARDSON J.A.
	CALDWELL S.J.		RIVIS P.L.
	CARTWRIGHT E.E.		ROBINSON W.J.
	CHEYNE J.		ROGERSON H.
	CLIFTON A.B.		ROSS G.
	COLLIER R.		RUDLAND L.
	COMRIE D.M.		SCOTT C.
	COX A.J.		SHANNON T.J.
	CREIGHAN J.C.		SYMES A.
	CREWS F.		THERON M.J.
	DAVIES T.E.		THOMAS E.
	DAVIS C.H.		TIERNAN T.
	DEVERNEUIL J.T.		TRAHARNE A.
	DICK F.		TURNER F.W.
	DONALD J.M.		TURNER J.
	DRISCOLL B.O.		TWYMAN W.H.
	DUNBAR F.D.		VAN ROOYEN J.
	EDWARDS T.		VICKERS G.
	FOGWELL L.R.		WARWICK J.
	FRANCIS A.C.		WILLIAMS A.E.
	GARDNER E.R.B.		WILLIAMS E.L.
	GLASS J.		WILSON C.
	GORING A.R.		WILSON H.
	GRAHAM J.		WINTER J.
	GRACEY H.L.		WRIGHT J.L.

Tpr.	WRIGHT W.J.		Bmdr.	LAWSON T.
	WYNNE E.C.			LEMEIRE J.F.
	YOUNG B.			McNAIR A.W.
				MILNE C.E.

Total of 1010 Awards

With Clasps - 878

No Clasps - 132

Notes:
L/Cpl. V.J.M. Christopher was killed in action 5.7.06.
Tpr. W.B. Griffin - The 1906 clasp was issued to him, loose, on a parade with the UMSINGA MILITIA Reserves (Roll 5)
Tpr. J.B. Skottowe had the clasp 1906 issued to him, loose, by ESTCOURT MILITIA Reserves.
It is of interest to see recorded Tpr. Orleans Prince A of:-

NATAL FIELD ARTILLERY
1ST BRIGADE STAFF
With Clasp 1906
Roll No. 16

Lt/Col.	PUNTAN H.H.C.
Capt.	EDWARDS G.O.
Sgt/Tpt.	YORK W.J.

No Clasps Issued

QMS	LOUTIT J.
Sgt/Cook	CHAPMAN C.

Total of 5 Awards

With Clasps - 3

No Clasps - 2

NATAL FIELD ARTILLERY
"A" BATTERY
With Clasp 1906
Roll No. 18

Maj.	WILSON C.
Capt.	BLACK W.J.
Lt.	ALMOND E.
	McINTOSH R.
RSM	CARSWELL J.E.I.
BQMS	EMERY E.
Sgt.Sad.	RIVENS S.A.
Sgt.Tail.	ROSE A.
Sgt.	BRASH J.
	DARBY J.E.
	FRANCIS B.J.
	HORNER R.
	STEAD N.O.U.
	WOOD A.T.
Cpl.CK	BENSLEY H.
Cpl.SS	GLEN G.
Cpl.Tpt.	TAYLOR E.D.
Cpl.	CLARKE E.H.
	LAMONT C.
	LYNE P.E.
	NICHOLSON H.
Bmdr.	KILMISTER F.A.
	KIRK H.B.
Bmdr.	LAWSON T.
	LEMEIRE J.F.
	McNAIR A.W.
	MILNE C.E.
	OWENS J.
	REDMAN C.H.
	VON MENGERSNAUSEN C.F.
Gnr.	BALLARD A.L.
	BIRD H.L.
	BOWEN W.P.
	DANIELS F.C.
	DOLTON B.
	FALCONER J.C.
	GENTLE R.L.
	HARPER H.
	HEAN E.A.
	HOWARD P.
	HUGHES G.W.
	IMRIE R.
	KEY C.
	LATHAM A.G.
	MATTHEWS M.
	McKENNA H.
	McNAIR R.
	MILNER C.
	MOORE F.H.
	MURCHIE J.
	MURRAY P.E.
	NICOLSON F.
	NYCE F.
	SCHOFIELD W.
	SCOTT T.
	SPERRYN C.P.
	TAGGART W.
	TAGGART W.J.
	THOMPSON H.J.
	TRUMAN R.W.
	WARD E.
	WARD G.R.
	WAUDBY W.H.
	WHITE A.
	WOODROFFE P.S.
Dvr.	ALLAN A.
	BAXTER A.H.
	EDEN F.
	FARMER R.C.
	FOLEY S.I.
	GRIFFITHS F.J.
	GUILLOD C.
	HARVEY G.H.
	KENNEDY T.E.P.H.
	LANCASHIRE W.
	LITTLE F.E.
	McDONALD W.
	MIDDLETON H.
	MILNE G.S.
	MOORE E.H.
	MOORE H.H.
	PAY C.
	PELLOW J.C.
	PERKS E.S.
	RATHBONE C.
	REEN B.
	SHAW C.J.
	SMITH H.F.
	STEWART W.
	WALDRAM H.D.
	WOOD S.
	YOUNG D.A.
	WHITE A.S.
Trpt.	STEPHENSON H.O.

No Clasps Issued

Lt.	D'ALMAINE H.A.A.
BSM	CAIN C.
SS.Farr.	GOVE W.
Sgt.WH	BROWN D.
Sgt.	GASCOYNE P.
	ROBB D.J.
	WULFF G.
Cpl.	PRICKETT F.C.
Bmdr.	GOOD W.
	YOUNG A.G.
Gnr.	ARMITAGE A.
	MacMILLAN R.
	SCOTT H.F.
	SMART E.W.
	TOWSERY F.H.
	WHEATLEY G.B.
	WOOD H.J.
Dvr.	CUSTANCE R.M.
	KILMISTER V.C.
	MACEY E.F.
	RALPH G.W.

Total of 115 Awards

With Clasps - 94

No Clasps - 21

NATAL FIELD ARTILLERY
"B" BATTERY
With Clasp 1906
Roll No. 19

Capt.	STUART J.
Lt.	ACUTT F.H.
	FARRELL J.L.
	FLETCHER J.S.
	JAMIESON J.S.
2nd Lt.	BENINGFIELD W.R.
Sgt.Maj.	PITCHER F.J.
BSM	REEN F.E.
BQMS	RICH K.
Sgt.Farr.	McGREAVEY J.C.
Sgt.Wh.	WILCOCKS W.T.
Sgt.	DIACK G.
	DOWNARD T.
	DUCKHAM J.W.
	MORRISON L.G.
	SLACK A.E.
	STANTON H.D.
	STUPPLE A.
	TAYLOR R.W.
Bomb.	ANDERSON A.
	DARL J.A.
	DOVE J.W.
	LINDSAY J.
	MAJOR H.
	PLUMMER A.
	WIGZELL H.A.
	YOUNG R.C.
Cpl.Sadd.	PHELPS R.J.
Cpl.SS	WRAY J.W.
Cpl.Trtr.	KIRSCHBERG M.B.
Cpl.	BICK F.S.
	BOWEN J.
	GODDARD A.
	GOY L.
	KING G.B.
	TOMLIN J.H.L.
Tptr.	GLOVER P.
	HARRIS E.J.
Gnr.	AMIS N.C.
	ANDERTON A.C.
	BARKER W.
	BARNES J.
	BODDY J.A.
	BRAYSHER C.
	BUCHANAN N.
	CLAYTON T.P.
	COOMBE V.G.
	COWLEY C.L.
	EMANUEL T.
	FABIAN D.J.
	GRIFFITHS G.
	GRIFFITHS W.H.
	HARMAN E.G.
	HEARSUM T.W.
	HORNE F.E.
	JOHNSTON A.
	JOHNSON H.W.
	JONES T.W.
	KING A.L.
	KIRK T.H.
	LOTT W.J.
	MARTIN W.J.
	MAJOR B.
	MAYES W.J.
	MOORE G.
	MURCHIE C.A.A.
	PURCOCKS G.F.
	REGNIER V.L.
	SLANEY S.D.
	SUDLOW A.V.
	VISICK V.
	WALKER H.S.
	WILSON N.E.
	WOODBURN W.R.
Dvr.	AULD A.E.
	CAIN H.
	CARRICK A.E.H.
	CORNISH W.T.
	CURRIE J.C.
	ECCLES G.G.
	GRACE T.H.
	HUGHES J.
	IRVINE J.B.
	JONES A. (289)
	JONES A. (430)
	LEDDRA G.
	LEVY I.
	McBAIN T.
	McLEAN J.
	MADDOCKS J.H.
	MOLE C.E.
	NICHOLLS H.E.
	PARTER A.W.
	RATHBONE C.
	SINGER H.A.
	STEPHENS J.M.
	SUTHERLAND A.
	TAYLOR R.
	WALMSLEY G.
	WHITE P.
	YORK J.

No Clasps Issued

Lt.	ING F.J.
Gnr.	ALCOCK F.
	CAMPBELL A.
	CLARK T.S.

Tpt.   PUNTAN H.

Total of 106 Awards

With Clasps - 101

No Clasps - 5

Note:
The Regimental No!s (although they do not appear on the medals) have been placed after the initials of those whose rank initials and surnames are the same.

NATAL FIELD ARTILLERY
"C" BATTERY
With Clasp 1906
Roll No. 4

Capt.	BIGBY W.S.
Lt.Hon.	
Capt.	PYBUS W.H.L.
Lt/QM	NICHOLLS G.R.F.
Lt.	BENNETT M.W.
	EADIE D.M.
	MURRAY H.
	RAWLINSON E.R.
RSM	BRACE T.
QMS	WYATT H.
Sgt.Collar Makr.	WOOD F.C.
Sgt.Farr.	McMANUS G.
Sgt.Whel.	ANDREW T.
Sgt.	ANDERSON P.
	DOWNES H.G.T.
	DRIVER G.E.
	JAMES L.E.
	RAWLINSON J.P.
	SPRATT N.C.
	STALKER J.D.
	WRIGHT W.S.
Cpl.	BENNITT W.O.
	CHAPLIN R.M.
	EDMONSTONE F.J.
	JOHNSTONE W.M.P.
	LINDSAY D.A.
	McCULLOUGH J.R.
	McKELLAR A.
	MASON O.
	PORTSMOUTH H.
	VALENTINE W.H.
Bmbr.	MASON W.H.
	MOODY W.H.
	RUNCIMAN S.E.
	SCOTT J.
	STEWART G.G.
Shoeing Smith	SALTER G.
Tmptr.	COOK J.C.
Gnr.	BARNES F.G.
	BARNES P.
	BEHRENS D.H.
	BRINKLOW H.J.
	DANIELS G.C.
	FLETCHER E.V.
	FRENCH F.H.M.
	HALLETT H.W.R.
	HERON J.
	HOSKEN S.V.
	HOVE J.A.

Gnr.	HUTCHINSON P.L.
	LANGLEY M.W.
	LEE S.S.
	McDOWELL J.D.
	MERCER H.
	MOUNTFORD H.J.
	PERKS J.J.
	POTTER F.H.
	RIDLEY A.C.
	ROGERS T.
	SQUAIRES W.J.H.
	WALKER J.C.
	WARREN T.
	WILLIAMS C.E.
	WILLIAMS W.E.
	WILSON C.
	WRIGHT O.R.
Dvr.	ANDREW A.S.
	ANDERSON W.H.
	BRIDGE F.W.
	CARBIS J.F.
	CHRISTIE H.G.
	GRAHAM G.
	HOLGATE R.A.
	HORNBY G.E.
	HOSKEN S.V.
	IRVING C.
	LETHERNE W.E.
	LINDSAY P.R.
	LORAM W.C.
	MacDONALD A.
	MACKINLAY W.
	MARSH C.W.
	McINTOSH R.
	McKENNA E.
	PATTON S.J.
	PRICE P.B.
	SAVILLE C.D.
	THRASH E.J.
	VON LEVETZOW A.F.T.
	VON LEVETZOW C.F.
	WILSON H.M.

No Clasps Issued

Maj.	CURRIE O.J.
Sgt. Collar Makr.	COOPER W.
Sgt.	STRONG J.C.
Bmbr.	DOWLING H.F.
	JAFFRAY W.A.
	PRATT T.A.
Gnr.	BELL H.J.
	WOLHUTER J.R.
Dvr.	BOYCE D.R.
	PLOWRIGHT R.E.

Total of 101 Awards

With Clasps - 91

No Clasps - 10

NATAL FIELD ARTILLERY
POM POM SECTION
With Clasp 1906
Roll No. 17

Lt.	SWAIN W.H.
2nd Lt.	BENINGFIELD C.J.
Sgt.	DUNDAS L.E.

Sgt. RASMUSSEN H.
Cpl. BURD C.S.
HUNTER J.W.
WOOD R.G.
Gnr. HARTLEY R.H.
HEALEY A.E.
KILMISTER M.H.
NOVICE
SERUSE R.G.
SMITHSON R.
WALLER W.C.
Dvr. ARMSTRONG H.J.
BELL G.
BROWN B.C.
CAMPBELL S.D.
DOYLE W.H.
LEFEVRE H.
MELLON H.F.
MITCHELL W.
VICKERMAN W.A.
Tpt. FORBES T.W.

Total of 24 Awards

With Clasp - 24

No Clasps - Nil

NATAL GUIDES
With Clasp 1906
Roll No. 56

Sgt/Maj. STONE W.I.B.
Sgt. ERNSHAW R.
MASON W.
STONE A.

Total of 4 Awards

With Clasp - 4

No Clasp - Nil

NATAL MEDICAL CORPS
With Clasp 1906
Roll No. 13

Maj. BALFE J.H.
BOWKER C.A.
BUNTINE R.A.
PLATT H.T.
Capt. AUSTIN ROBINSON F.
CRASS C.H.
DE GROOT SVR.
GORDON CUMMING G.
HOWDEN R.K.
LEA C.E.
LOOS W.C.
MASSER C.
MILNER SMYTH R.
MOBERLEY G.K.
PEARSTON M.G.
PEVERLEY W.A.
ROSS J.M.
WATKINS PITCHFORD W.
Lt. ARMSTRONG H.W.
RSM POWELL O.E.
Sgt. ARTHUR R.T.N.
BAGNALL G.P. MSM

Sgt. CROSS A.H.
FARLAND W.J.
GREENFIELD A.
LAZARUS L.
LE FEBOUR A.J.
MacMANUS W.
NESBITT J.F.
WILLIAMS J.H.
Cpl. ADAMS A.W.
ARTHUR W.R.
BRADLEY A.E.
CALVERT A.E.
CROOKS J.S.
CURRANS J.
EMERTON F.
FRASER C.
LITTLE E.F.
LYON R.
MARKS J.
MAY W.
McDONALD J.
MILL A.
ROBERTSON P.R.
WILLIAMS C.T.
Pte. ABEL G.
ADAMS F.W.
ANDERSON A.E.
BALMER D.
BARRIE P.
BARTON G.D.
BECK A.W.
BECK H.T.
BELL M.
BELL W.
BRENNAN J.
BYRNE J.
CLARKE T.E.
COX G.
CRABTREE W.
CROOK W.T.
DANIELS J.
DEANE J.E.
DEELY W.
DEWAR W.
DRAPES G.R.
DRUMMOND J.
ELFORD S.H.
FLETCHER R.
FULLER E.
GESHAM M.
GILBERT J.
GRAINGER R.
GREEN A.
HALL W.
HARRISON T.
HILTON R.
HUNT T.
HUNTER J.
IRWIN J.C.
JONSON O.
KAINE A.
KITE K.
LAURENT G.
LITTLE J.J.
LONG J.H.
LOVELL H.
MARSHALL H.
METTERS W.
MORTON D.A.
NAUGHTIE J.A.
NELSON F.

Pte.	PEASE D.C.
	SHEFFIELD A.
	SIDLE H.
	SLYTH B.
	SMITH J.
	THOMPSON H.P.
	THOMSON J.
	TREGEMBO J.
	TUCKETT S.P.K.
	WARWICK G.C.
	WREN C.

No Clasps Issued

Capt.	BOOTH CLARKSON J.
	CROZIER G.R.
	GILMOUR J.C.
	LIVINGSTONE F.I.
Cpl.	SEARS C.W.
Pte.	ANDREW F.G.R.
	COHEN L.
	EDGE D.W.
	GUEST M.
	MacINTOSH A.
	McKAY J.
	MIDDLETON D.
	NORMAN H.
	NOWELL T.H.
	ROBERTS G.
	SHAPLAND F.
	STOKOE J.
	STRANGE C.H.
	WARWICK C.C.

Total of 123 Awards

With Clasps - 104

No Clasps - 19

NATAL MILITIA STAFF
With Clasp 1906
Roll No. 2 & 58

Col.	BRU-de-WOLD H.T. CMG DSO VD
Lt/Col.	HYSLOP J. DSO VD
	LUGG H.
	TAYLOR D.
	WALES A.T.G.
	WATKINS-PITCHFORD H.
Maj.	BLEW T.
	CHOLES F.J.
	WILSON R.W.
Capt.	BOSMAN W.
	FORBES A.J.
	HOSKEN C.V.
	INMAN R.I.
	LAWRENCE S.R.
	TANNER W.E.C.
Lt.	BURT W.A.J.
Staff	
Sgt/Maj.	ANDERS F.A.
	BLANEY J.H.
	HOLLAGHAN J.
	OLDS W.
S/Maj.	BODGER E.
	FIELD J.W.
	GLEAR W.
	ROBINSON C.A.
	SHELL J.H.
QMS	POTTER B.

S/Sgt.	BOND B.C.
	COLLINS J.G.
	COWPER W.H.
	GILLAM J.

No Clasps Issued

Maj/Gen. DARTNELL Sir J.G.

Total of 31 Awards

With Clasps - 30

No Clasps   - 1

NATAL MOUNTED RIFLES
With Clasp 1906
Roll No. 21

Lt.Col.	MURRAY-SMITH W.
	SPARKS H. VD
Hon.	
Lt.Col.	RITCHIE J. VD
Maj.	SMITH W.H.
Cap/Adj.	HURST G.T.
Cap/Paym.	GARBUTT A.L.
Capt.	ARMSTRONG R.
	CAMPBELL W.A.
	KNOX A.G.
	RATTRAY P.M. DSO
	STUART R.B.
Lt/QM	CARMONT P.
Lt/Bandm.	GIBB G.R.
Lt.	BELLVILLE H.W.
	BLAMEY A.H.G.
	GIBSON G.D.
	MIRRLEES W.J.
	SMITH W.H.
2nd Lt.	ADDISON P.
	ALEXANDER W.G.
	ARMSTRONG A.L.
	BLACKHURST R.
	KETLEY W.G.
	LANDSBERG C.J.
	MUNRO J.D.
	SPARKS H.F.
	THOMPSON R.W.
RSM	CAGE J.E.F.
Sgt.Maj.	PAYNE G.R.
S.Sgt.Maj.	ENSOR-SMITH P.
	FLOOD J.J.
	JAMIESON A.P.
	SCHWEGMANN W.
Or.Sgt.	HURST H.H.
SQMS	ALCOCK J.W.
	GARBUTT H.B.
	HURST C.J.
	KNOX L.E.
Farr QMS	ORCHARD W.G.
Sgt.Cook	KURZ J.
Sgt. Farr	DINGLEY J.
	SCOTT W.
	STEVENSON F.J.
Sgt.Sadd.	BULL H.
Sgt.Trump.	BIBBY W.H.
Sgt.	BAZLEY F.C.
	BRANSBY W.S.
	BROWN J.
	CARMONT G.
	DOWNS A.R.
	FITZGERALD T.O.

Sgt.	FRARA M.S.		Tpr.	ABREY R.
	GEERDTS M.			ADAMS A.
	HULME J.R.			ADAMS H.V.
	KIRK C.W.			ADAMS M.
	KONIGKRAMER A.H.			ALEXANDER C.M.
	McINTOSH C.E.			ANDERSON E.
	NAGLE D.M.			ANDERSON J.A.
	PAY W.H.			ANDERSON O.
	POLKINGHORNE R.T.			ARGO H.
	PRICE C.E.			AUSTIN H.C.
	SANDER A.F.			AYERS F.R.
	SCHWEGMANN H.H.			BAKER A.G.
	SMITH H.E.			BANKS P%
	SPEARMAN E.W.			BARNES E.W.
	STARR A.W.			BARRETT J.
	STEWART C.			BATTEN A.T.
	SWALES C.C.			BAUMAN J.
	TEDDER R.F.			BAYTOPP A.
	THORNBURGH A.			BAZLEY E.V.
	THRING J.F.			BAZLEY S.H.
	WADMAN A.J. MSM			BEALL R.W.
	WARDALE S.E.			BECK C.
	WAYNE G.H.			BECKER G.R.
	WERNER F.			BEGHIN C.H.
	WHITE H.W.			BELCHER M.
	WILLMOT E.H.			BIBB F.
Cpl.SS	ERRINGTON J.			BIGNOUX W.
	ROBINSON T.B.			BINGHAM T.
Cpl.Trump.	TOMLINSON C.L.			BINGHAM W.D.L.
Cpl.	ACUTT R.L.			BOHMER H.G.
	ADDISON H.			BOND F.W.
	ALEXANDER A.B.			BOSCH W.A.
	BALCOMB H.R.			BOWEN E.
	BAYTOPP E.A.			BOWER T.R.
	BIRD J.E.			BOWMAN E.
	BROWN M.			BRADSHAW A.
	CAMERON A.M.			BRANSBY R.A.
	CONYNGHAM D.B.			BRAY J.B.
	COUCH R.			BRISTO J.
	DALES G.N.			BROOKS A.H.
	DAVIDSON W.C.			BROWN J.
	DICKENS C.F.			BROWN J.W.
	FINCH J.B.			BROWN W.A.
	GRICE A.			BRUNSKILL F.K.
	GRINSTEAD J.B.			BILKELEY C.F.
	HALL R.S.			BURKE F.W.
	HAMMOND J.M.			BURMAN H.S.
	HARVEY E.R.			BURNS C.J.
	HUNTER W.			CARLETON H.G.
	JONES J.H.			CARTER R.W.
	KNIGHT F.H.			CARTWRIGHT L.
	KOSTER J.			CASSIDY D.
	McEWAN W.			CHAMBERLAIN J.H.H.
	PEARSON R.G.			CHAMBERLIN H.
	RAMSAY C.B.			CHILDS W.M.
	RICKERBY I.			CLARK A.H.
	SCHAFERMANN E.H.			CLARK A.M.H.
	SCHWEGMANN C.H.			CLARK H.C.
	SCHWEGMANN H.F.			CLARKSON F.C.
	SIMPSON A.G.			CLODE H.A.
	SPARKS G.S.			CLOWES W.
	SPEARMAN G.C.R.			COKER W.
	STEVENSON E.F.			COLE J.
	VOLK C.			COLENBRANDER L.
	WESTERMAYER A.W.			COLLINGHAM A.M.P.
	WINSON C.F.			CONYNGHAM L.H.
	WRIGHT W.T.			CONWAY A.J.
Trump.	BOWEN R.W.			COOK J.M.
	DAVIDSON J.P.			COOMBES S.
	FREESE J.			COONEY J.
	MORNING C.			COOPER A.J.
	TOSEN H.J.			COX A.W.

Tpr.	COX H.C.	Tpr.	JACKSON T.E.
	CRUICKSHANK J.		JAMES G.F.
	DAINTREE A.B.C.		JARDINE C.D.
	DALGETY G.		JARVIS H.J.
	DANIEL A.V.		JENNER J.
	DANIEL J.S.		JOHNSON A.W.
	DENNISON J.R.		JOHNSON W.
	DICKENS A.W.		JOHNSTONE J.H.
	DOBBIN J.		KEACHIE A.
	DONALDSON J.		KEMP W.G.
	DORE G.R.		KEMPTHORNE J.
	DUGUID P.A.		KENNEDY M.
	EDWARDS D.R.		KETTLE E.B.
	EDWARDS R.		KYLE R.
	EGAN W.G.		LAMOND J.P.
	ELLISON J.B.		LANCASHIRE C.
	ENGLISH C.H.		LANGE H.F.R.
	ENSELL G.		LEE J.W.
	EVANS J.		LE MESURIER H.G. MSM
	FIELD C.H.		LEWIS A.K.
	FIELD T.S.P.		LOGAN A.A.
	FITZGERALD A.W.		LOGAN A.C.
	FLETCHER H.M.		LOGAN B.R.
	FLORENS C.		LOGAN H.W.
	FRASER H.B.		LUKE E.P.
	FREAKES B.		LUMSDEN J.
	FREEMAN W.J.		MacGUIRE W.
	FROST D.		MacNEILLIE W.S.
	FYNNEY F.		MANNING J.K.
	GALLAGHER G.		MASON P.A.
	GARDINER A.E.		MATHESON J.D.
	GARLAND E.S.		McDONALD J.
	GELL E.H.T.		McGREGOR E.
	GELZAR A.		McIVER D.
	GIBB A.M.		McKENZIE L.
	GIBBS W.		McLEOD R.
	GIBSON E.T.		METHERELL P.H.
	GILLITT E.B.		MILLARD H.V.
	GOODWIN W.E.		MILLER C.A.W.
	GOULD A.A.		MINTO G.
	GRANT J.H.		MITCHELMORE F.G.
	GRAYSON T.		MONEYPENNY E.M.
	GRIGG W.H.		MORGAN M.B.L.
	HAGER J.		MORTON H.M.
	HAMLYN T.		MOWAT G.
	HANLON J.		MOWAT W.J.
	HARBOTTLE J.W.		MULCAHY H.W.
	HARBOTTLE T.R.		MUNRO A.C.
	HARPER A.H.		MURPHY C.D.
	HATCH R.B.		MURPHY M.
	HATCHELL F.		NICOLSON W.H.
	HAYS N.I.		O'LEARY T.
	HAZELL J.B.		OLSEN M.A.
	HECKLER H.H.		ORME F.J.
	HENDERSON T.		ORMOND A.I.
	HIGGS C.H.		PACKER O.
	HILL W.H.		PARKER W.J.
	HILMER W.		PAUL W.
	HINDE A.H.		PEARSON T.G.
	HITTLER G.		PIERCY J.E.
	HOFMEYER B.		PINNOCK J.D.
	HOGAN J.		PIRRIE A.
	HOLDEN W.		PIZEY R.
	HOLLISTER R.		PLATT H.
	HORNE P.C.		POCKLINGTON T.J.
	HORNING H.W.		POPE W.
	HORWITZ B.		POTTERILL W.
	HOSKING H.		POWELL A.
	HUDSON J.		PRESTON W.G.
	HUNT E.W.		PRICE P.A.
	HUNT J.A.P.		RANS T.
	HUTSON F.E.		RAYMOND F.

Tpr. RICHARDSON H.
RICKERBY A.
RITCHIE F.W.M.
RITSON E.
ROBERTS A.G.
ROBERTS C.J.
ROBERTS F.W.
ROBERTS S.L.
ROBERTSON A.W.
ROBERTSON S.W.
ROBINSON A.C.
ROBINSON W.
RODGERS M.
RODGERS M.H.
RUDGE A.
SALMON A.G.
SANDER E.F.W.
SANDER F.A.
SANDER H.C.J.
SCHAFERMANN W.H.
SCHWEGMANN F.
SCHWEGMANN H.C.
SHEPHERD C.J.
SIME ALBERT
SIME ALEX
SIMPSON A.
SIMPSON J.A.
SJOBLOM I.E. MSM
SKINNER F.J.
SMITH C.
SMITH C.E.
SMITH E.S.
SMITH H.H.
SMITH R.H.
SMITH W.
SNOWDEN T.D.
SPARKS V.G.
SPENCER W.J.
SPRUIJT G.
STEILL J.
STEPHEN J.J.
STEVENSON A.W.
STUHR H.
SWALES A.
SWINDELLS F.
SWINDELLS T.H.
SYKES A.C.
TEDDER A.H.
THOMAS R.H.
THOMPSON J.
THOMPSON J.D.
TILL F.
TILL T.J.
TILL W.
TURNER S.R.
TYMMS A.
URQUHART J.
VAHL H.E.
VENNING C.G.
WALSH J.J.
WARD J.C.
WARDALE C.H.
WARREN C.P.
WATSON R.J.
WAUGH V.S.
WAYNE R.
WELDON V.
WELLS T.
WEST L.
WHITEHEAD W.R.
WILKINSON A.H.
WILLIAMS G.A.

Tpr. WILLIAMS J.T.M.
WILLIAMS T.
WILMOT A.F.
WILLS W.M.
WILTSHIRE W.
WIMBOURNE S.
WOLHUTHER A.P.
YOUNG K.N.

Attached to Natal Mounted Rifles

Lt. PRAED G.A.M.
5th Light Infantry Regiment Indian Army On furlo (Sic) from own Unit. Received Medal with clasp. It appears that the medal could be named to his Indian Army Regiment.

No Clasps Issued

Maj. HENWOOD C.
Lt. STEWART G.
SSM PAUL A.
Sgt. HAYCROFT J.C.
PULFORD C.
Cpl. RYCROFT C.
Tpr. ALEXANDER C.R.
ASH G.V.
ATTLEE W.H.
BARR P.F.
BRICKHILL T.F.
BULL E.G.
BULL W.G.
BURNS F.J.
CARTER R.W.
CHUDLEIGH G.H.
CRISP A.J.
DOUGALL G.J.
DOUGALL J.
GOODEN T.A.
KING W.M.
LONDON A.
MADDOCK R.H.
McDONALD N.
McKENZIE J.
MEDHURST F.M.
MURPHY J.
NICHOLSON W.
RATTRAY W.
SHOESMITH W.
SOBERMAN J.
TEAGUE P.W.
THORNTON E.
WHITEHEAD H.
WILLEY C.E.
Trump. PERKS L.W.
SMITH G.A.

Attached to Natal Mounted Rifles

Capt. KNOWLES G.A.
2nd Lancers (Gardner's Horse) Indian Army Received the Medal without the clasp. On furlo (Sic) from his own Unit. It appears that the medal could be named to his Indian Army Regiment.

Total of 462 Awards

With Clasps - 424

No Clasps - 38

Note: Tpr W.G. Bull Died on Service
          Tpr. A.J. Crisp Died on Service
          Tpr. A. Powell Killed in Action

NATAL NATIVE HORSE
With Clasp 1906
Roll No. 30

In this roll the Surnames and the Christian names are shown, for instructions to this effect, accompanied the Original of the Roll submitted. The first name is the surname.

Maj.	MOE GEORGE B.O.
Capt/Adj.	SAMUELSON ROBERT C.A.
Capt.	McCORD J.B.
L/QM	OLIVER J.B.
LT.	COMRIE PIETER A.
	KIRBY GEORGE F.
	LUGG HARRY
	MULLER WILHELM J.H.
	POPE HAROLD
QMS	ANFIELD CARLYLE
	HOWARD H.L.
Sgt.	AMSTERDAM ADAM
Chief	HLONGWANA TABHANE
	MINI STEPHEN
Sgt/Maj.	GULE NAPHTHALI T.
	MOLIFE STEPHEN
	SOPELA WALKER
QMS	HLONGWANA HLELETWA
	MALINGA PETROS M.
	MSIMANG ENOCH
Farr.Sgt.	PARDY T.A.
Sgt.Revd.	MDOLOMBA E.
Sgt.	CELE MICHAEL
	DHLAMINI CHARLES
	HLATYWAKO CHARLIE
	HLONGWANA DILI
	HLONGWANA MKIZE
	HLONGWANA NGIDI
	HLONGWANA SIDWEDE
	KUMALO ALFRED
	KUNENE ABRAHAM
	MANKO EPHRAIM
	MKWANANZI MICAH
	MINI WILLIAM G.
	MKIZE ISAAC F.
	MOLIFE JAMES L.
	MTEMBU ROBERT
Cpl.	DHLADHLA NICOLAS
	DHLAMINI GEORGE
	GAMA BENJAMIN
	GULE EBENEZER
	GUMEDE BHEBE
	HLONGWANA MAHLANYA
	HLONGWANA MAQOMFI
	HLONGWANA MBHOBHO
	HLONGWANA MBITOLISA
	HLONGWANA NGWENYANA
	KHABA SIBHAMU
	KUNENE PAKADE
	MABUZA AMMON
	MAHLOBO TOMOTHY
	MDHULI TSHAKA
	MLAMBO SILULWANE
	MLAMBO ZINTO
	MNGADI SAMUEL
	MPETWANE SIMON
	MPINGI BHULIRAU
	MTUNZELA ZEBULON
Cpl.	MTYALI MZWILI
	MVELASE DAVID
	NCAWANA ALFRED
	NTOMBELA ABEDNEGO
	RADEBE WILLIAM
	SILAMLELA JOHN
	XABA STEPHEN
	ZIKODE NDHLUYENGWE
	ZIKODE SIYEPU
	ZONDO MBAMBONDE
	ZONDO MDHLUDHLU
	ZONDO MPAPU
Tpr.	CELE PHILEMON
	CILIZA VIVIAN
	DAZELA MKOKWANE
	DHLADHLA MANGUZA
	DHLADHLA MANYONI
	DHLAMBULA NDHLOMUNTU
	DHLAMBULA TSHAWUTSHAWU
	DHLAMINI BHONSA
	DHLAMINI GININDA
	DHLAMINI GXOLODO
	DHLAMINI MAPOVELA
	DHLAMINI MASONDO
	DHLAMINI NDAYELA
	DHLAMINI SALIMANI
	DHLAMINI WILLIAM
	DUMA BENNETT
	DUMA GEBA
	DUMA NQOLENI
	GASA SOPALAPALA
	GOLI MANZODIDI
	GRIEVE DAVID
	GULE LAZARUS
	GULE SIBHALO
	GULE SIMON
	HLABAKOMBELE MAGOBOLA
	HLATYWAKO CAKIJANA
	HLATYWAKO FENTELE
	HLATYWANE FUSI
	HLATYWAKO GUMGUMU
	HLATYWAKO MDWEBU
	HLATYWAKO MGIQIKA
	HLATYWAKO MGQIBELO
	HLATYWAKO MHLOPE
	HLATYWAKO NDONJANA
	HLATYWAKO NGAZANA
	HLATYWAKO NOMKOKOKO
	HLATYWAKO NONGOBELO
	HLATYWAKO QUANDA
	HLATYWAKO SIGODO
	HLONGWANA CAMSELA
	HLONGWANA CITSHOLO
	HLONGWANA DAYIMANA
	HLONGWANA DHLABANTU
	HLONGWANA DHLAMBUZI
	HLONGWANA DUKWANA
	HLONGWANA FINELA
	HLONGWANA GQOMU
	HLONGWANA JAKALASE
	HLONGWANA MAQHAQHAZELA
	HLONGWANA MBHEMI
	HLONGWANA MDABULA
	HLONGWANA MFUNZANA
	HLONGWANA MGEDHLE
	HLONGWANA MKOKO
	HLONGWANA MKONTYWANA
	HLONGWANA MSEBENZI
	HLONGWANA MZIMUBI
	HLONGWANA MZIYONKE
	HLONGWANA NDHLELA
	HLONGWANA NKATA
	HLONGWANA NTSHOLWANA

Tpr.	HLONGWANA PELE	Tpr.	MDAKANE MBALENI
	HLONGWANA SIGIDI		MDAKANE MCITWA
	HLONGWANA SIMAHLA		MDHLULI GENDANE
	HLONGWANA SOMPUNGANA		MDHLULI NKANI
	HLONGWANA TSHWELE		MDHLULI PATI
	HLOPE MKOLWANE		MDHLULI PIET
	KAMBULE DANDAYI		MEMELA NCAYI
	KAMBULE SOLOMON		MGUNI JOSEPH
	KANYILE MTWALO		MGWABATSHE MWELI
	KESWA LANGABI		MHLANGA MEHLOKAZULU
	KESWA MBHODHLELANA		MHLANGA NDAVU
	KOZA MABIZELA		MHLOPE NDODA
	KOZA MAPOVELA		MIYA MPENDU
	KOZA MGENI		MJWARA NGEQE
	KOZA MVUSENI		MKABELA HARRY
	KOZA NTYIBONGO		MKABELA HENRY
	KOZA NTYUMAYELO		MKALIPI NTENGO
	KUBHEKA FRANK		MKISE NTAMBO
	KUBHEKA MTSHUMAYELI		MKIZE NATHAN
	KUMALO CHARLES		MKIZE SAMUEL
	KUMALO DAVID		MKONZA WILLIAM
	KUMALO DICK		MKULISI NGANGEZWE
	KUMALO ESAU		MKWANANZI AARON
	KUMALO HEZEKIAH		MKWANANZI ADAM A
	KUMALO JAMES		MNDEBELE JAMES
	KUMALO JOLIET		MOLIFE ALFRED A
	KUMALO MADHLUPE		MOLIFE JAMES
	KUMALO MFINYELI		MOLIFE NATHANIEL
	KUMALO MKONTO		MOLIFE OBAAS
	KUMALO SIMON		MOLIFE SIMON
	KUNENE ANDRIES		MOYA HENRY
	KUNENE GWEGWANA		MPETWANE MPIKWA
	KUNENE JOHN		MPINGI JANA
	KUNENE MAHAULANA		MSIMANG JOSEPH
	KUNENE MBULAWA		MTALANA NAKENI
	KUNENE SOLOMON		MTEMBU BUSHA
	KUNENE WILLIAM		MTEMBU JALI
	LAFLEUR BOIZANA		MTEMBU GQOYI
	LAFLEUR EDWIN		MTEMBU TOBIAS
	LANGA GENDANE		MTUNZELA JOSIAH
	MABASO MTSHOLOLO		MTYALI STOFFEL
	MABASO ZACHARIAS		MTYALI WANDU
	MABUZA PHILIP		MVULA MANDHLA
	MADHLALA JOHANNES		MVULA MBAYIMBAYI
	MADHLALA JOHN		MVULA MPINI
	MADHLALA SOLOMON		MYENI MALAU
	MADUNA SAMUELS		MZINYANE CHARLIE
	MAGWAZA JONAS		MZINYANE HOBE
	MAHLOBO DAYIMANA		MZINYANE NQEQE
	MAHLOBO MESE		NCUBE ELIAS
	MAHLOBO YEDWA		NDABA BULULU
	MAHOBO MPANZA		NDABA GAPA
	MALINGA NDHLOVU		NDABA GIBA
	MALINGA SIMON		NDABA MAGEDHLE
	MALINGA WILLIAM		NDABA MBORWENI
	MANZINI MALIBENI		NDABA NOZAZA
	MAPANZELA NONKOBOTSHE		NDABA SAHLUKANISO
	MAKIKANE JOHN		NDABA SIKUKULA
	MASIKANE STRONGONE		MDABA SILEVU
	MASONDO JOHANNES		NDABA TSHEVU
	MATEBULA WILLIAM		NDHLELA AARON
	MATI MBALEKELWA		NDHLOVU ALFRED
	MATI MNIKINA		NDHLOVU AMON
	MAVUSO ISAAC		MDHLOVU MASHIKEYANA
	MAZIBUKO MAHLALELA		NDHLOVU SIKOTA
	MBAMBO HLANZENI		NDHLOVU SIMON
	MBATA DHLANSI		NDHLOVU STOFFEL
	MBATA MPIKA		NDIMANDE JOEL
	MBATA MXABANISI		NDINISA MHLAHLO
	MBELE FANA		NGCOBO ELIAS
	MBENSE MPIKWA		NGCOBO THOMPSON
	MBHABHAMA MTETWA		NKABINDE JACOB
	MBHANJWA MTIMBENI		NKALA SIMON

Tpr. NKOSI AARON
NKOSI JOSEPH
NKOSI MPIYAKE
NKOSI SIMAHLA
NTOMBELA FRANCIS
NTOMBELA MYENGWA
NTONDOLO NQOBOKAZI
NTUMBA TSHUBA
NXUMALO JOHANNES
NXUMALO JOHN
NXUMALO SOLOMON
RADEBE JAMES
RADEBE JONAH
RADEBE MANGANDENI
RADEBE TALASI
SIKAKANE ALBERT
SIKONDE MALLWA
SIRHULE SAMUEL
SISHANGE MAJUMBA
TAHLA BHODHLELA
TSHABANGU MHENDO
TSHANGASE MEHLWANA
TSHELEMBE MUNA
TWALA MAKUBALO
VILAKAZI JOBANE
XABA ALFRED
XABA MBOTSHWA
XABA MPELENGU
ZIKODE MANGQUZU
ZIKODE MGAULI
ZIKODE MTIYA
ZIKODE NDHLEMBE
ZIKODE SILEVU
ZONDO BAHALA
ZONDO GOGOLOLO (245)
ZONDI GUNDU
ZONDO KIMBILI
ZONDO MAGUTSHWA
ZONDO MARUBULWANA
ZONDO MDONSWA
ZONDO MEYI
ZONDO NGUNGUNDHLOVU
ZONDO MNINIMUZI
ZONDO MNYAMAWENDHLU
ZONDO MPIYAKE
ZONDO NDHLELENI
ZONDO NDHLAMVUZO
ZONDO SILEVU
ZONDO TAKATI
ZULU MPITSHIZA
ZUMA PHILIP
ZUMA XESIBE
ZWANE GWAISA
ZWANE MAHOIZA
ZWANE NCEZU
ZWANE NTINI
ZWANE SENZENI

No Clasps Issued

Tpr. KUENE MASHACK
NKABINI MLULAMA
TAHLA MDUDU

Total of 338 Awards

With Clasps - 335

No Clasps - 3

Note: The Medal to Tpr. Gogololo Zondo appears twice on the original Roll - the Regimental Nos. identical, - but only one medal appears to have been issued.

NATAL NAVAL CORPS
With Clasp 1906
Roll No. 20

Lt.Cmdr. HOARE F.
Gnr.Off. BRUCE R.G.
Lt.Paym. BARTLETT J.F.
Lt. CHAMPION O.
Sub.Lt. BROWN R.E.
HILLIER F.M.
HULSTON C.F.
W.O. SKINNER T.
C.PO. JEWITT C.W.
P.O.1 ANTHONY W.
FRY W.
GOULDING A.C.
JOHNSTON W.
KIRK C.S.
LEWIS H.
STEAD R.E.
P.O.2 AMBLER G.
CAMPBELL A.W.
CAMPBELL J.W.
COOMBES J.A.
DICKINSON R.C.
DICKSON F.N.
DUNN A.
HOUNSELL H.J.
MANN D.B.
RICKS A.
STRACHAN G.J.
P.O.2 Writer CARNABY J.
ChiefCarpt. Mate. POOLE H.
Chief Stew. DUNCAN A.
Lead Seam. BARON I.
BRASH D.
CHISHOLM T.M.
DAVIS S.L.G.
MURCHIE H. McC.
McKENZIE C.T.
NANNESTEAD O.
REID A.
SPRATT L.
STRACHAN S.
TOWHEY M.
WALKER A.H.
WHITELAW C.O.
WIGZELL J.L.
CGI FRANCIS E.M.
GI STRACHAN C.
JOHNSTON J.F.
Bugl. SMITH A.W.
Singl. BURTON M.C.J.
Seamn. ASTRUP W.J.
AUSTIN J.
BALLARD A.C.
BLOXHAM G.H.
BONEHILL C.
BONEHILL T.
BRADLEY G.E.
BROWN A.M.
BROWN C.S.
BROWN H.J.
BROWN J.N.
BUCHANAN N.D.D.

Seamn.	BUSH T.T.W.	Seamn.	WHITE A.H.
	CANNON F.J.		WILSON W.H.
	CAUDLE E.W.		WOOD H.F.
	CRADDOCK G.C.		
	CUMMING A.		

No Clasp Issued

Lt.	FORRESTER
P.O.2	HARMER G.T.
Lead Seamn.	LITTLEJOHN A.H.
Buglr.	WILKINSON T.L.
Seamn.	AGNEW J.

	CUNNISON J.A.		AXEN C.
	DANIEL F.		BARRETT J.
	DICKSON J.H.		BELL A.
	DUFF S.		BRADFORD H.
	DUNNING J.		BROWN J.B.
	DUTHIE R.		BUCHANAN D.
	EASTERBROOK H.P.		CAPPONI P.
	ELSTON A.V.		COKELEY T.
	EMERY F.		COLLINS T.
	FISHER B.W.		COLQUHOUN A.
	FLETCHER F.L.		COOPER R.D.
	FORD A.T.		CUNDY J.
	FORD H.		DATES A.
	FRANCIS F.C.		DEAN J.H.
	FRASER J.C.		DOHERTY E.P.
	GANDY W.H.		DORN M.
	GILL J.B.		ELLIS W.J.
	HARBOTTLE R.T.		ERICSON L.
	HARBOTTLE W.L.		FISHER H.
	HARDWICKE H.H.		FOLEY G.
	HIRST J.W.		GODFREY A.
	HOLT L.		GOODMAN F.
	JENNINGS D.J.B.		HAMILTON W.P.
	KEMP G.		HANNAN E.
	KENRICK S.		HARRIS H.
	KIDD J.		HASLAM E.
	KIDNEY J.		HEDLEY G.
	KIRK C.		HICKMAN C.H.
	LANDER L.		HILL T.
	LEE J.W.		JOHN N.
	LEE W.H.		JOHNSTONE W.H.
	LINDUP E.C.		KING J.
	LOMAX J.		LANDSELL E.
	MACK B.W.		LAWRENCE J.
	MACKAY C.O.C.		LINDEROTH C.
	MARCUS J.		LINDSAY W.
	MASON J.B.W.		LOVETT T.
	MAY H.J.		LYDIATE A.
	McDONALD J.R.		McKAY W.
	McDOUGAL R.		MERCER E.
	McKENZIE D.		MILES J.W.
	McKENZIE J.		MORGAN E.
	MITCHELL H.D.		MORGAN W.
	MITCHELL J.B.		MORIN C.J.
	MITCHELL W.G.		MORRIS A.
	MOWATT C.		MUNROE J.F.
	MURCHIE T.		NEWMAN C.
	MURGATROYD P.		NICHOLSON T.
	MURPHY M.		OLDS A.
	NEWMAN C.C.		PEARSON W.
	NORTH A.H.T.		PITT J.
	OGILVIE R.J.		RILEY T.
	PEARCE W.L.		ROFFEY F.
	RATCLIFFE H.S.		ROGERS G.
	RICHARDS J.		SAYERS W.
	RONBECK J.		TUNNY J.
	ROWE W.H.		TURPHY J.
	SALTER H.F.		WAKE D.
	SCOTT E.G.		WALKER T.
	SHAND G.T.		WALSH M.
	SHARP W.		
	SHEPPARD J.		
	STEVE H.		
	TOUHEY T.		
	TRUNLEY J.J.		
	WARD J.E.		
	WARD S.C.		

Seamn.	WHITE A.E.		Lt.	SHERRELL E.
	WRIGHT H.			WHITE E.F.W.
			RSM	BROWN E.W.

Total of 203 Awards

With Clasps - 136

No Clasps - 67

NATAL POLICE SUPPLEMENTARY
No Clasps Issued
Roll No. 44

Sub.Insp. HUNT S.H.K.
Tpr. ARMSTRONG G.

Total of 2 Awards

With Clasps - Nil

No Clasps - 2

Note: Sub.Insp. S.H.K. Hunt and Tpr. G. Armstrong - Killed at Byrnetown on 8th February 1906
It was the murder of these two Police Officials that precipitated the Rebellion.

NATAL POLICE
With Clasp 1906
Roll No. 32 & Supplementary

Col.	MANSEL GEORGE	CMG
Lt.Col.	CLARKE W.J.	
	MARDALL G.S.	
Maj.	BOUSFIELD W.	
	COLLYER J.B.	
	DIMMICK O.	
	EARLE W.E.	
	FAIRLIE C.E.	
	GEORGE W.C.H.	
	IVES W.E.	
	LYTTLE W.E.	
	MARSHALL J.B.	
	MEINERS L.H.U.	
	PHILLIPS E.L.	
	PRENDERGAST A.	
	ROSE J.E.	
Capt.	BANISTER A.A.	
	BELL R.A.	
	BROWN H.R.	
	CLIFTON A.S.	
	EVANS F.	
	HAMILTON J.	
	HELLET H.R.	
	LEWIS C.W.	
	MATRAVERS W.T.	
	MAXWELL R.S.	
	OTTLEY C.R.	
	WEST H.H.	
Supt.	SMITH J.F.	
	McDONALD W.	
	BARRY W.	
	BLAKE E.P.	
	FOTHERGILL R.	
	JOHNSON J.D.	
	LINDSAY C.R.	
	McARTHUR J.	
	PINTO L.A.	

Lt.	SHERRELL E.	
	WHITE E.F.W.	
RSM	BROWN E.W.	
	INGLE W.	
CSM	CLARKE H.A.	
	GAZZARD H.J.	
	GRAHAM A.D.	
	GUTRIDGE J.T.	
	PERCEVAL C.J.	
	WILLIAMS C.	
	YOUNG A.J.S.	
BM	HUGHES E.P.	
QMS	FISK E.E.W.	
1c Sgt.	ALLAN R.	
	BATTERBURY J.	
	BECKETT J.	
	BELL R.	
	BORGNIS A.H.	
	BUTLER J.W.	
	CALDER J.W.	
	CAMINDA L.	
	CUMMINGS J.G.	
	GRIMALDI S.	
	HATTRILL G.	
	HAWKES J.	
	JANES F.	
	KERRIDGE S.H.	
	LANE S.	
	LEMPRIERE H.L.	
	LYNCH J.	
	MACKAY F.C.	
	MANN W.	
	MARTIN S.H.	
	NEWSON G.P.	
	NEVILLE H.C.	
	PURDON E.H.	
	ROBBINS C.D.	
	ROBERTS A.	
	STEPHENS W.H.	
	STURGEON C.J.	
2c Sgt.	ARCHER C.L.	
	ATTWOOD S.H.	
	BARHAM H.C.G.T.N.	
	BARNES J.H.	
	BELCHER F.H.	
	BLUNDELL E.G.	
	BRITTAIN F.	
	BROWN E.T.N.	
	BRUCE J.A.	
	CAMPBELL H.A.	
	COUPE P.	
	COURT G.F.	
	CREYDT B.	
	FISHER C.G.	
	FOLKER O.L.M.	DCM
	FRENCH S.	
	GEORGE N.H.	
	GORDON D.B.	
	GRAHAM G.S.	
	GUEST C.W.	DCM
	HARKE W.H.	
	HAYES W.R.	
	HOLWAY W.H.	
	KENNY T.T.	
	KER R.H.	
	L'ESTRANGE E.W.	
	LETHBRIDGE H.F.H.	
	LOWE E.L.	
	LUTLEY E.	
	MacPHERSON C.G.	
	MALLISON A.E.	
	MANSEL E.	

2c Sgt.	MARGETTS C.B.	L/Sgt.	TULLIDGE T.W.H.
	MARTIN H.W.		WARD H.
	MARTIN R.		WILSON H.R.
	MEGSON F.		WILSON M.E.
	MELLICK R.		WRIGHT C.W.
	MICKELBURGH H.T.	A/Sgt.	JACKSON W.
	MORGAN H.S.S.	Pm/Sgt.	MACANDREW E.
	MURPHY W.	Farr/Sgt.	MEARES W.J.
	NIXON G.	Det.	BALLENDEN G.
	OPENSHAW A.H.		BLISS F.J.
	PHILLIPS J.S.		CARR F.H.
	RATHBONE F.		CHEETHAM J.E.
	REDGROVE E.E.		CLARKSON J.S.
	REHMANN D.		CLAUDE P.
	REYNOLDS A.		COHEN W.
	REYNOLDS W.A.		CRADDOCK J.W.
	SCHAFER K.A.		CUFF A.J.
	SEED R.		DETTLING C.
	SMITH J.		EDDY W.T.
	SMITH T.B.		GRANT R.
	STEPHENS F.W.		HARMSFORD R.W.
	TERRY E.G.		JOHNSTONE R.
	TOMS J.H.		LOVEROCK R.M.
	WATSON C.J.		MILLIKEN W.J.
	WEBB W.J.		NEILSON C.W.J.
	WEVELL J.		STEVENS R.E.
	WHITEHEAD G.S.		THEUNISSON A.G.
	WILKINSON F.L.		TRANSCHELL F.G.
	WOODGATE C.		TUFFS A.W.
L/Sgt.	BATCHELOR A.H.		VERINDER H.E.
	BICHENO F.		WALKER F.V.
	BLACK W.		WALSH R.
	BOWMAN J.M.		WYNNE-COLE H.C.
	BOWYER J.M.	Con.	BANKS G.M.
	BRICKDALE M.		BEARD W.F.
	BROWN T.		BELL L.G.
	BULLER C.J.		BEST C.H.
	CARTER A.A.		BOYD J.
	COLLIS W.J.		BRANDON H.E.B.
	CURTIS F.L.		BROD J.C.E.
	CUSACK J.W.		BROWN R.
	DURANTY P.H.		BUSH A.E.
	EDWARDS W.F.		BUTLER H.E.O.
	FARRELL P.		CROSSE V.C.
	FREEMANTLE H.A.		DAVIS T.
	GEORGE R.S.		DIAMOND M.
	GIBBS A.		ELSTON F.T.
	HARRISON J.C.G.		HALL C.
	HOLMES J.		HAYES G.E.
	HOMFRAY D.H.C.		HENRYS J.L.
	KENNEDY F.		HICKMAN J.
	LANDSBERG C.P.		HILL J.F.
	LARPENT A.J.		HILLS H.
	LEVICK F.F.		HOOPER F.
	MATTHEWS C.W.		JOHNSON A.
	MOORE J.P.		KINSEY A.
	MOULE M.C.		LIBBY R.
	NOTMAN C.M.		LOUCH R.C.
	OTT F.H.		MAJOR C.F.
	PAGE F.G.		MOSSMAN C.
	PHILLIPS J.P.		MURPHY T.
	POPHAM J.K.		O'NEILL H.
	PYNE R.I.		RENNIE S.
	REFAULT G.H.		ROBEY J.
	REMNANT C.H.		ROCHE H.
	RODDY G.		SLINEY T.
	ROGERS H.P.		STOCKDALE F.R.
	ROTHON P.J.		THOMPSON W.
	SMITH A.H.		TIETY A.
	STEWART P.H.		TORLAGE J.F.
	STRINGER T.W.		WALKER C.E.
	TUCKER N.		WAREHAM T.

Con.	WATKIN J.F.	Tpr.	BRANIGAN G.P.J.
	WILLE C.W.		BRANDON G.E.
	WILLIAMS F.		BRANKEN J.C.
	WILLIAMS F.J.G.		BRAUEL T.
	YOUNG R.		BRIDGES C.
Tpr.	ADAMS J.W.		BRIDGEWATER C.
	ALDERSON F.B.T.		BRIGGS T.
	ALKIN T.A.		BROMLEY J.E.M.
	ALLAN W.H.S.		BROOKES J.
	AMBROSE A.		BROWN C.A.
	ANDERSON L.B.		BRUNKER L.
	ANDREWS A.V.		BRYANT J.C.
	ANLEY V.R.		BUCHAN H.W.I.
	APPLEYARD J.W.		BURCHAM L.M.
	ARMOUR R.		BURMESTER W.
	ARNOLD G.W.		BURNE A.T.
	ARNOLD H.W.		BURNETT W.
	ARNOLD N.		BUTLER A.V.
	ARNOLD R.H.		BUTLER H.
	ARNOTT W.A.		BUTLER R.B.
	ASHTON A.H.		BUTTS J.
	BAILIE A.B.H.		CAMERON D.S.
	BAINES W.		CAMERON W.T.
	BAKER F.		CANTLEY V.C.
	BALLANTYNE R.		CARDEN D.
	BALLANTYNE W.H.		CARGILL T.F.
	BALLINGTON G.		CARROLL J.
	BARNES J.		CARTER E.H.W.
	BARR W.A.		CARTER F.
	BARRETT A.F.		CARTER G.G.
	BARTON H.J.		CARTWRIGHT C.
	BASKETT R.		CARTWRIGHT F.
	BASTON J.J.		CASEY H.V.
	BATEMAN G.		CATLING B.N.
	BATTERS J.		CHALLIS G.A.
	BEARD E.F.		CHAMBERS R.R.
	BEATTY H.		CHANLEY C.E.
	BECK J.A.		CHATTAWAY W.H.
	BECKLEY P.G.		CHEADLE W.
	BEECHER F.F.T.L.		CHENEY R.H.
	BELL J.W.		CHIOLE F.D.
	BELL R.		CLARK E.K.
	BENHAM C.E.G.		CLARKE C.
	BENNETT H.S.N.		CLARKE F.L.
	BENSON H.		CLARKE H.W.
	BERGQVIST G.		CLARKE P.F.
	BERRY D.		CLIFFORD H.
	BEST H.D.		CLOVER A.W.
	BEST N.P.		CLOVER G.R.
	BEVERLEY R.		COCHRANE D.E.
	BICK J.G.		COLE A.
	BISHOP W.		COLLARD W.
	BLACK D.M.		COLLINS A.W.
	BLACKBEARD J.		COLLINS E.F.
	BLACKBURN E.R.		CONNOLLY J.J.
	BLANCHE J.J.C.		CONQUEST G.
	BLOW L.		CONYNGHAM J.E.
	BOARDMAN H.		COOK R.W.
	BODDY H.O.		COOKE A.B.
	BONNER J.		COOKE D.
	BOOTH A.		COOKE G.H.
	BOOTH R.W.		COOKE G.W.
	BOOTN T.		COOKE J.V.
	BORLASE F.H.		COOKE S.S.
	BOSCHEN F.		COOPER L.
	BOSSE G.T.		COOPER R.C.B.
	BOUTLER H.P.F.		COOTE J.
	BOWEN G.B.		CORCORAN F.W.
	BOWYER C.H.		COUSIN F.
	BOYLE T.		COX G.W.
	BOYNE E.		CREAGH J.G.
	BRADLEY W.P.		CREDIE D.J.

Tpr.	CREED J.W.	Tpr.	FOX F.S.
	CROUCH F.		FOX H.J.
	CULLUM J.H.		FRAMES E.D.
	CUTHBERT A.		FRANKFORD A.
	DADSON F.H.		FRANKISH A.E.
	DALE T.L.		FRANKS W.E.
	DALE W.W.		FRASER D.
	DALY E.H.		FREEMAN H.F.
	DATE A.		FREEMANTLE P.
	DAVIDSON F.G.		FREER A.H.
	DAVINIERE L.C.F.		FRERE O.G.
	DAVIES A.W.		FREW R.
	DAVIES T.B.		FULLFORD C.J.
	DAVIS H.G.		GADD H.M.
	DAVIS L.		GALE J.E.
	DAWKINS C.S.		GALT H.V.
	DAWKINS R.S.		GARDE C.J.
	DEACON G.W.		GARDINER S.D.
	DEANE T.G.		GARDNER J.F.
	DELPORT J.		GARLAND E.F.H.
	DE ROS D.		GARRETT H.M.
	DE SARIGAY V.		GASCOIGNE W.
	DEWIS T.S.		GASCOYNE B.W.
	DIBBEN J.W.		GAT C.W.
	DICK A.		GEE A.
	DICKS W.J.		GIBBONS F.
	DICK-CLELAND L.		GIBBS A.J.
	DICKENSON E.G.		GIBBS E.W.
	DORE G.H.		GIELINK J.R.
	DORNEY T.F.		GLAISHER E.B.
	DOVE H.C.		GLASSPOOLE G.A.B.
	DOWLING P.C.		GLYNN T.
	DOYLE S.		GOATLEY E.T.
	DRUCE F.L.		GOBERT P.
	DUMPHREYS W.J.		GODFREY V.J.
	DUNN F.A.		GOODMAN A.L.
	DURHAM P.R.		GOODWIN F.H.
	EARDLEY T.T.		GOODWIN G.J.
	EDEN F.E.		GOODWIN J.
	EDMESTON G.A.		GORDON M.
	EDMUNDS W.T.		GORE S.N.
	EDWARD H.W.		GOULSTONE J.U.
	ELLIOTT C.E.		GRAHAM J.A.
	ELLIOTT H.W.		GRANT D.J.S.
	ELLIS O.		GRANT T.E.
	ELTON A.E.		GRAY C.
	EMANUEL J.		GREEN F.D.B.
	ENNSLIN L.		GREEN H.A.
	EVANS A.E.		GREEN J.H.
	EVANS A.S.		GREGORY A.
	EVANS A.W.		GREENWOOD J.P.
	EVANS W.F.		GRIFFITHS M.J.
	EVETTS H.		GRIFFITHS R.G.
	FALECKI A.		GRIFFITHS T.E.
	FARR H.S.		GRIMSDELL A.H.
	FARRINGTON A.J.		GRIX C.E.
	FARRINGTON G.E.M.		GROOME J.J.
	FEARON J.C.		GROVE R.B.W.
	FENNER H.H.		GUEST J.G.
	FENWICK O.E.		HAACK G.E.A.
	FERGUSON D.		HADOW H.C.
	FERGUSON F.		HAIG T.F.
	FINCH T.H.		HALDER F.H.
	FINLAY R.H.		HALES V.C.
	FITZPATRICK S.		HALEY J.
	FLOOD C.P.L.		HALEWOOD H.
	FLOWERS M.H.		HALLORAN E.S.
	FOLEY R.W.		HAMIL M.
	FORD W.E.		HAMMOND C.E.
	FOSTER C.F.		HANCOCK F.S.
	FOTHERGILL J.C.		HARDING S.J.

Tpr.	HARWICKE C.	Tpr.	KEMP J.M.
	HARGREAVES P.D.		KETTLE H.
	HAROLD H.		KEYSERLINGK Von. C.
	HARPER W.		KIDSON F.W.
	HARNSON H.W.		KINDER G.
	HARRAWAY D.		KING T.
	HARRIS J.		KIRKTON J.
	HARRIS T.W.		KNIGHT J.
	HARRISON H.W.		KNIGHT R.C.
	HARVEY J.		KNOTT W.K.
	HASLETT S.		KNOWLES A.C.
	HATMAN G.		KOCH R.C.
	HAWKEN M.		LAING R.
	HAWNEY F.H.		LANE J.C.A.
	HAYES H.H.		LANG T.G.
	HAYES R.P.		LANTMAN J.
	HAYMES H.C.		LARMOUTH J.M.
	HEARN A.		LAVIN H.
	HEDGES T.H.		LAWLER G.H.
	HEWITT G.A.		LAWRENCE A.R.
	HEYBOURNE W.		LAWRENCE J.
	HICKMAN C.S.		LAWSON E.
	HICKSON H.W.C.		LAWSON F.K.
	HILLS A.		LEAN A.W.
	HILL E.P.		LEAN H.E.
	HODGE G.G.		LEAROYD F.
	HODGENS W.V.		LEASK H.G.A.
	HOGAN J.P.		LEASK H.S.
	HOGAN T.		LECHLER W.I.A.
	HOLBROOKE G.H.		LEE R.J.
	HOLMES F.		LEE T.H.
	HOLMES T.		LEES SMITH A.B.
	HOLT G.S.		LEGGATT G.
	HORSLEY R.G.C.		LEITCH A.F.
	HORSWELL H.D.		LE ROUX S.J.
	HOUNSOM C.H.		LEWIS A.E.
	HOUSDEN H.F.		LEWIS W.L.
	HOWARD N.		LIDWELL G.
	HOWARTH M.B.		LITCHFIELD H.
	HUGHES E.		LOFSTROOM S.H.
	HUGHES W.T.		LOGAN G.L.
	HUMPHREYS N.S.		LOGNON T.W.
	HUNT H.G.		LOKER D.G.
	HUNT R.H.		LOKER W.J.
	HURST G.H.R.		LONG J.T.
	HYLAND E.D.		LONSDALE G.
	IEVERS H.F.		LORD A.S.
	JACKSON W.		LOVEKIN A.B.
	JACOBS R.A.		LOWDER H.W.
	JACOBSON O.R.		LYONS A.H.
	JAMESON W.R.		MacKENZIE G.K.
	JEAPES H.R.		MADDICK S.A.
	JENSEN C.		MAGILL W.D.
	JEWELL E.A.		MAINWARING E.C.L.T.
	JOHN W.		MANN E.O.
	JOHNSTONE C.E.		MANNING H.
	JOHNSTONE D.J.		MARSHALL F.H.
	JOHNSTONE J.		MARTIN C.W.
	JOLLIFFE H.		MARTIN E.S.
	JONES A.		MASSEY H.
	JONES F.		MATHER W.A.
	JORDAN J.A.P.		MATHEWS W.
	JORDAN W.A.F.		MATHIAS C.R.
	JURY F.		MATHIESON A.
	KATON A.		MATHIESON B.H.
	KEARNEY J.		MATHIESON J.
	KEARNEY J.J.		McAFFER J.
	KELLY G.W.		McALPINE H.
	KELLY J.		McCABE C.
	KELLY M.L.		McCAULL W.
	KELSEY E.W.O.		McCONACHIE J.A.
	KEMP C.M.		McCUTCHAN E.H.

Tpr.	McDONALD C.J.G.	Tpr.	PALMER J.H.
	McDONALD J.A.		PARFREY C.
	McDOUGALL P.R.		PARKHOUSE J.L.
	McEWAN S.J.		PASSMORE W.E.
	McGILLIVRAY G.H.		PATTERSON G.R.
	McGILLORAY J.		PAY F.
	McGINLEY J.T.		PEARSON J.E.
	McGONEGAL M.		PEEL F.E.H.
	McGOWAN B.		PELLISSIER W.
	McGREGOR R.F.		PEMBERTON H.
	McINTYRE D.		PEPPERCORN O.
	McKAY W.B.		PERRYMAN A.J.G.
	McKENZIE A.W.		PEYTON G.A.
	McKENZIE E.J.		PHILLIPS J.
	McKEOGH W.		PHILLIPS P.R.
	McKEOWN J.J.		PIETERSE T.J.
	McLEAN A.		PITMAN E.
	McLEAN G.H.		PLATT J.K.
	McLEOD J.		POLTE T.G.
	McLEOD R.		POPHAM F.
	McLOONE T.P.		PORTER C.J.S.
	McLOUGHLIN E.E.		PORTER T.
	McMASTER E.S.		POTGIETER A.M.
	McNAB H.D.		POTGIETER P.M.
	McPHEE J.H.		POTTER J.
	McQUADE J.		POTTS J.K.D.
	McROBERTS B.A.		PRICHARD L.D.
	McWILLIAMS G.B.		PRICHARD O.W.
	MEYER B.J.		PURCHELL J.
	MICHELL F.E.C.		PYNE G.W.
	MICHELSON O.		PYNE O.M.
	MIDDLETON L.		QUIGLEY A.
	MILEHAM L.		RAINSFORD R.F.
	MILL W.J.		RALPH S.A.
	MILLER J.L.		RAMSEY H.G.J.
	MISKEN L.H.		RAVES H.S.
	MOFFITT W.M.		REDINGTON D.C.
	MONGER M.		REID A.
	MOODIE D.		REID H.A.
	MOORE C.W.		REISE G.H.
	MOORE G.B.		RENNETT J.A.
	MOORE J.		RICE W.P.
	MOORE J.F.		RICHARDSON J.
	MORONEY T.E.		RICHARDSON T.W.
	MORIN E.		RILEY A.W.
	MORRIS H.		RIPPON H.A.
	MORRIS V.E.		RIVETT CARNAC C.G.
	MOSS R.C.		ROBEY G.S.
	MOTNERSOLE L.W.		ROBERTS A.H.
	MOULE F.H.F.		ROBERTS F.C.
	MUIR W.J.		ROBERTS J.H.
	MUNROE J.		ROBERTS P.
	MYATT T.A.G.		ROBERTSON J.
	NEAVE E.A.		ROBINSON A.
	NEILSON N.V.		ROBINSON D.
	NEWMAN H.A.		ROBINSON P.
	NICHOLL A.B.		ROBINSON T.
	NICHOLSON S.		ROGERS F.T.
	NICKOLS P.		ROSEBY P.R.
	NORVAL A.D.		ROSENQUIST F.
	NUNN W.G.		ROSS A.
	NUTMAN T.S.		ROSS M.E.
	O'CONNOR P.		ROWE R.R.
	OLDFIELD T.F.		ROWLAND A.E.
	OLIVE G.		RUDD A.
	OLMESDANL F.		RUMBLETON W.
	ORR R.S.		RUTHERFORD T.
	OULTON H.C.		RYAN P.W.
	OWEN G.F.		RYDER L.S.D.
	PAGE W.		SABINE A.
	PAKENHAM J.A.		SALE A.
	PALMER G.		SALTER J.

Tpr.	SANDBROOKE G.	Tpr.	SWEETAPPLE F.H.
	SANDLEY G.H.		SYKES E.
	SANDYS E.		TABERHAM A.E.
	SATCHWELL A.C.		TAIT N.
	SAWTELL J.R.		TALBOT F.J.
	SCARISBRICK G.F.		TALMAN S.A.R.
	SCHONBURG A.C.		TAYLOR W.
	SCHORN J.P.		TERBLANCHE J.C. (3647)
	SCHULTZ H.		TERBLANCHE J.C. (3649)
	SCOTT F.G.		TERBLANCHE J.J.
	SCOTT J.		TERBLANCHE S.F.
	SCOTT J.W.T.		TERBLANCHE W.S.
	SEARANCKE F.A.		TETLOW F.
	SELLS A.J.		TEW D.
	SEWELL F.W.		THOMAS A de B
	SHANNON A.		THOMPSON J.
	SHARPE H.E.		THRELFELL G.R.
	SHAW A.F.		THRING F.C.
	SHELDRICK A.H.		TIDBOULD G.G.
	SHELL J.H.		TORBITT E.S.
	SHEPPARD R.		TORPEY F.A.
	SKINNER J.M.		TOWNSEND C.J.
	SLADE W.		TREANOR T.T.
	SLATTERY W.		TRIGG J.H.
	SLATTERY W.H.		TRIGGS O.D.
	SLOAN A.W.		TRIMMER A.H.
	SMART A.J.		TRUMBLE R.W.
	SMART P.H.		TUCKER H.R.
	SMART S.		TULL F.J.
	SMEETON H.		TURNER E.A.
	SMITH C.		TURNER J.
	SMITH E.G.H.		TURNER W.
	SMITH E.P.		TWEEDIE P.
	SMITH G.J.L.		TYLER E.F.H.
	SMITH H.A.		TYRELL A.E.
	SMITH J.		UNDERWOOD S.
	SMITH P.A.F.		UNDERWOOD W.
	SMITH T.W.		USHER A.
	SMITH-BROOK G.A.		VAN AARDT F.W.
	SMYLY E.M.		VAN DE BERGH J.J.
	SMYTH D.J.F.		VANDERPUMP S.N.
	SNELGROVE A.J.		VAN RENSBURG P.J.
	SNELGROVE W.		VAN ROOYEN C.J.
	SPALDING G.		VAN VUREN P.S.
	SPENCE H.		VAN VUREN W.F.
	ST.JOSEPH A.		VERDON P.
	ST.JOSEPH R.		VILJOEN C.
	STAFFORD T.		WADDINGTON G. O'N.
	STAKES G.		WAKEFIELD F.
	STANFIELD A.		WALLER C.R.
	STEGALL S.		WALLER F.C.
	STEVENS F.		WALLIS R.G.
	STEWART A.		WARD A.H.
	STEWART E.D.		WARREN F.D.
	STEWART W.M.		WATSON A.E.H.
	STILL T.P.		WAUCHOPE L.
	STOCKS W.C.		WELLS W.B.
	STOKES O.H.		WESSELS H.J.
	STONEBANKS D.		WESSELS J.J. (3455)
	STRAFFON W.G.		WESSELS J.J. (3873)
	STRATFORD WINGFIELD M.E.J.		WEST W.S.L.
	STRAND E.H.		WHATELEY F.
	STRANGE R.F.		WHEATLEY G.
	STRATTON G.		WHEELER A.J.
	STUART J.D.		WHELAN R.J.
	STUART L.A.		WHITE A.W.
	STUCKEY R.C.		WHITE C.H.
	STYLES G.		WHITE F.J.
	SUTHERLAND N.D.O.		WHITE W.
	SUTTON W.H.		WHITELOCK C.E.
	SWANN A.E.		WHITTAM J.W.
	SWARBRICK J.		WHITTY J.

Tpr.	WHYTE A.D.	Tpr.	KINCADE G.
	WILKINS G.G.		LOVEROCK E.M.
	WILLETT H.G.		LOWE A.E.J.
	WILLIAMS J.		MABY S.H.
	WILLIAMS W.F.M.		MAHON R.
	WILLIS A.E.		MARTIN E.J.
	WILKS A.B.		MARTIN W.B.
	WILLSON W.		MARVELL A.
	WILSON D.		MASSON L.E.
	WING J.W.		MAUGHAN G.H.
	WINGFIELD H.J.		McCOACH J.A.
	WINTER G.N.		MILLS T.P.
	WINTERBOER W.		MOLYNEUX F.H.
	WISE F.W.		MORTON T.
	WISEMAN F.N.		MULLEY W.
	WOOD A.A.		MURPHY H,
	WOOD F.T.		PEMBERTON A.
	WOOD W.T.		PHILLIPS C.
	WOODLEY P.A.		PICKERING W.R.
	WOODS H.		PILLING W.
	WOOF S.J.		PRATT A.W.H.
	WOOLEY J.D.		ROBERTS W.F.
	WOOLLEY J.H.		ROCHE H.
	WRIGHT T.H.F.		SANDER H.W.
	WYNCH F.		SCHOENTJES H.
	YEAMAN D.		SCHULTZ F.
	YEATMAN O.		SCOTT W.
	YOUNG A.		SHEPHERD H.O.
	YOUNG J.R.		SHERIDAN J.
	YOUNG W.F.		SHUSTER M.
	YOUNGHUSBAND C.		SMITH J.
Tmptr.	KING-MASON C.G.D.		SPALDING A.
	MILTON C.R.W.		STEWART D.
Wdr.	ALEXANDER C.C.M.		SWANN P.
	ANDREWS F.C.		TAYLOR H.W.
	BECK D.A.		TUOHY P.
	BEKKER F.J.		VILJOEN J.
	BIDDULPH T.H.		WHEELER T.R.
	BROWN A.J.		WOOLLEY R.
	BUCKINGHAM H.		
	BURKE J.	No Clasps Issued	
	CAREY F.W.		
	CHANDLEY A.B.	2cSgt.	HAYES W.R.
	CLIFFORD E.E.	Tpr.	ANNETTS R.
	COOPER B.		ARNOLD E.F.
	COOPER J.W.		BAKER J.W.
	CRAWFORD J.		BASS H.
	CUMING J.B.		BRANWHITE H.
	DAWSON T.		CAMPBELL S.D.
	DENHOLME T.		CONNOLLY J.M.J.
	DOWNES J.C.		CRAWFORD A.H.
	DOYLE D.		FERRIS R.S.F.
	DRAPER S.J.		GRAHAM H.
	EASTWOOD C.		JOHN D.
	ELGIE R.H.		LUCAS R.
	FARLEY A.E.		McCULLEY M.
	GOODWIN F.		McIVER W.R.
	GORDON A.		MORLEY J.F.
	GRAY J.		PAULS W.J.F.
	GREEN H.		PICOT G.W.
	GREENFIELD G.		POSNER H.M.
	GRIFFIN W.		POWELL E.H.
	GRIFFITHS A.F.		RANKING G de L.H.
	GRIFFITHS L.J.		SCOTT J.
	HALVORSEN H.		VOSPER S.C. St.C.
	HARRIS H.	Con.	HALL J.
	HUMPHREYS A.C.		HICKMAN J.
	HUNT J.P.	Wdr.	JOHNSTONE F.H.
	HUTCHINSON L.		JOHNSTONE G.T.
	JEFFERIES P.		McDONALD S.
	KELLY P.J.	Nat-Con.	LUNJANGA NGUBANE

Nat-Con. MALANGONKE MALINGA
SONSUKWANA BBUTU
TYALI MALINGA

Total of 1114 Awards

With Clasps - 1082

No Clasps - 32

Killed in Action
Tpr. A.H. ASHTON
2cSgt. E.T.N. BROWN
Tpr. J.P. GREENWOOD
L/Sgt. J.C.G. HARRISON

Note: Wdr. A. Gordon, appears twice on the original Roll. Only one medal, however, appears to have been issued.

NATAL POLICE GAOLERS
With Clasp 1906
Roll No. 43

Maj. SMITH A.M.
THOMSON J.R.
Capt. DEANE D.
Sgt.Wdr. DAVIES E.G.
HOWARD H.R.
KELLY R.
LIGHTENING C.S.
MOORE L.J.
SMITH H.M.
WADE F.
Warder DURBRIDGE W.
MORONEY P.
REID E.H.
SHANLEY P.
Gaoler BELL A.C.
BRANSGROVE S.A.
BRITTAIN E.
BURTON J.
CLARKE J.H.
COX A.B.
CULVERWELL J.F.
DARLOW G.A.
DAVIES J.
DEISTER J.
DELVIN J.H.
DONGLANDS R.F.
DUNCAN G.A.
ELLIOTT A.B.
ELLIS H.S.
GORDON J.X.
GRESSMAN P.W.
HEARN W.H.
HUSBAND A.J.
JENNINGS H.
LEWIS J.H.
LIGHTENING E.D.
MOFFIT C.
NOTT C.
O'NEILL A.E.
PARSONS W.F.
PHILLIPS W.J.
POUNDER G.H.
POWER Le P.J.A.
SILVA M.J.B.
SPEED H.
SPIERS R.
SWANN H.J.S.

Gaoler TAYLOR E.A.
TURNER F.E.
WILKINS W.E.

Total of 50 Awards

With Clasps - 50

No Clasps - Nil

NATAL RANGERS
With Clasp 1906
Roll No. 35

Lt.Col. DICK J.
Maj. BOYD-WILSON A.B.
FURZE J.J.
NICOLAY G.W.
Capt/Adj. SCHULLER O.
Capt. DICKSON J.
FORSBROOK C.M.S.
HOGG H.F.
LINDEMERE A.
MILNE A.S.
SMYTH J.W.
SUTHERLAND J.A.
WESTBROOK L.J.
WHITEHEAD J.J.
Lt. ALEXANDER W.A.C.
BLAKEMORE P.H.J.
BOWSER H.A.
BYNG H.R.
CAMPBELL A.J.
CARTER E.J.
DAVIDSON E.G.
DAY L.A.
DEVENISH J.
DOUGLAS J.G.
HARVIE W.L.
HEARNE F.G.
HEYWOOD A.
HIGHET F.B.
HOLMES-a-COURT R.A.
MARGARY A.F.
MEDICOTT R.F.C.
MORGAN J.
NORTHCOTT C.A.
O'SHAUGHNESSY W.W.
PHILLPOTT F.
PORTER C.P.G.
RICHARDS W.
ROSS T.H.
SIMPSON W.J.
SLOAN O.W.
SMITH A.G.
STERN P.T.
TALMAN S.A.R.
WESTON E.T.
YOUNG B.
RSM NEWSHAM R.M.
Col/Sgt. COWAN R.
DUNKLEY W.G.
EDWARD W.R.
KEIGHTLEY H.E.
LEWIS T.S.
MILLS E.W.
MULCASTER G.C.
SMITH C.H.
SMITH H.
WILLCOCKS W.G.O.
S/Sgt. COOMBES C.R.

S/Sgt.	EBBUTTE W.
	READE E.
Bugle/Sgt.	LAWLESS J.M.
Pay/Sgt.	EVANS J.C.
Sgt.	ALLISON A.E.
	BOOTH N.
	COONEY J.
	CRAIGEN W.
	CROFTON F.
	CROSS R.E.
	CUNNINGHAM J.
	DIXON R.
	DOHERTY J.A.
	DOMONE C.
	DUNN J.C.
	FLETCHER A.
	FORD J.
	FULLER W.F.
	GOODMAN A.H.
	GOUGH W.T.
	GREEN G.
	GRIFFITHS G.
	HALL T.F.
	JACKSON F.E.
	KING C.
	LASALLE C.A.B. De-
	LEWIS T.
	MACKAY J.G.T.
	McCANN J.
	MELLUISH A.G.
	MOONEY J.O.E.
	NELSON D.H.
	PEARSON L.E.
	PENNY W.L.
	POMFRET P.R.
	ROBERTSON J.B.
	ROLLO A.
	SPENCE J.H.
	TODD P.B.
	TURNER W.
	VIBERT C.A.
	WILLIAMS H.
	WILSON W.
	WOOD P.
	WORBY F.H.
Cpl.	ALLEN J.
	ARLINGTON J.
	BAND D.
	BAND M.
	BANTING W.E.
	BARBER G.I.
	BARWICK W.
	BRADLEY J.A.
	BRICKHILL W.
	BYRNE P.
	CAITHNESS F.R.
	CAMPBELL D.
	CAMPBELL K.
	COLLIN A.J.
	CORCORAN A.
	COWIESON T.
	CUNNINGHAM J.
	DERBYSHIRE G.
	DIXON F.E.O.
	DIXON S.
	DORAN W.
	DOWALL G.T.
	EMSLIE J.D.
	ENGLISH J.H.
	FARR C.
	FARRINGTON F.J.
	FISHER H.
	FLEURY F.J.
Cpl.	FOX H.
	GARNER T.H.
	GILCHRIST J.
	GILHAM C.L.
	GOODE J.
	GRAHAM R.P.
	GRAVES J.P.
	GREENLEES T.
	GRIFFIN J.
	HALL J.H.
	HARDING F.
	HIGGINS A.
	HINDLE P.
	HOLT E.C.
	HUTCHINSON M.J.
	JOHNSON W.
	LAWSON J.
	LESLIE H.S.
	LEYSON J.
	McCARTHY J.D.
	McILLWRAITH D.M.
	MORRELL F.A.
	MORRISON G. (278)
	MORRISON G. (19)
	MOWATT A.H.G.
	MULLINS J.
	NOLAN H.
	NORDWALD D.
	OSBORNE G.A.
	PLUMSTEAD R.
	RAMSDEN G.W.
	REX E.D.
	RUSSELL J.E.
	SAUNDERS W.
	SCOTT W.
	SHEEHAN C.
	SHEPPARD F.
	SHORTEN T.J.
	SIMPSON A.
	SOLE W.J.
	STOLLARD S.
	SYMONDS M.C.
	TAUNT E.D.J.
	THORNTON G.
	TODD D.
	TURNER C.W.
	UBEE O.
	VARIAN W.P.B.
L/Cpl.	ADAMS T.W.
	BLABER A.H.
	GREIG D.
	SNOWBALL R.W.
	WADE W.H.
Bugler	BURRAGE J.E.
	CHAMLIN A.F.
	CURRAN L.A.A.
	WOODHOUSE W.
Pte.	ADAMS A.R.
	ADAMS C.W.
	ADAMS J.
	ADAMS T.M.
	ADAMS W.E.
	ALDER H.F.
	ALDER J.
	ALLEN P.
	ANDERSON C.
	ANDERSON J.
	ANDERSON J.M.
	ANDREWS H.
	ANGER S.
	ANSCOMBE S.
	ARCHIBALD W.
	ARMITAGE G.L.O.

Pte.	ARMSTRONG J.	Pte.	CAVANAGH E.
	ARMSTRONG S.		CELLARIUS T.J.
	ART G.		CHAPMAN E.H.
	ATKEY P.J.		CHAPMAN J.
	ATKINS F.W.		CHAPMAN P.
	ATTWELL O.		CHEESEBOROUGH H.
	BAKER B.J.		CHEETHAM F.G.
	BAKER F.J.		CHEYNE D.
	BALL D.J.		CHILTON T.M.
	BALL H.		CHOTE A.S.
	BALLS J.T.		CHRISTIE A.W.
	BAPISTE W.		CHRISTIE N.
	BARLOW T.		CLARK G.
	BARNES J. (45)		CLARKE C.M.
	BARNES J. (360)		CLARKE G.F.
	BARRY W.J.		CLARKE J.L.
	BARTLEY A.		COKELY D.
	BATCHELOR H.		COLE A.
	BATCHELOR T.W.		COOKE J.A.
	BATTEN F.		COLEMAN T.
	BAULCH F.		CONNEFF J.
	BAYS R.		CONNOLLY J.J.
	BAXTER H.		CORMACK A.
	BEACOM R.		COULTER H.J.
	BEATTIE S.		COWEN H.M.
	BEAVAN J.C.		CRACKNELN D.
	BECKETT A.C.		CRAIG W.
	BEGGS F.		CRANNA A.S.
	BELL R.		CRANSTON J.
	BELLHOUSE J.		CRAWFORD J.I.
	BELT H.		CRAWFORD W.
	BENDER C.H.A.		CRAWFORD W.L.
	BENNETT E.D.		CREESE A.F.
	BILBY J.F.		CREWS F.
	BLACK A.J.F.		CUBBON J.A.
	BLOOM S.		CULLEN G.
	BLUE H.		CULLEY H.R.
	BONNING J.C.		CUNNINGHAM J.
	BOSCHER H.P.		CUNNINGHAM J.E.
	BOWEN W.		CURRAN C.
	BOWERS J.H.		CURRAN P.
	BOYLAN J.		DAGLISH W.J.
	BRADFORD W.W.		DAGUIN C.S.
	BRAY M.		DALE C.H.
	BRAZIER J.		DALEY P.
	BRENMER T.		DALY P.
	BRIEN W.		DANIEL F.
	BRITTON N.		DANN F.
	BROOKS S.J.		DARLING W.
	BROUGH W.		DAVIDSON F.
	BROWN B.B.		DAVIDSON G.
	BROWN J.A.		DAVIES G.
	BROWN J.N.		DAVIES J.E.
	BROWN T.		DAVIES S.
	BROWNE A.R.I.		DAVIS H.
	BROWNE W.		DAVIS J.
	BROWNING J.		DAWSON W.
	BRUETON A.N.		DESPARD G.W.B.
	BURKE R.P.		DEVEREUX J.
	BURNETT F.H.		DEWAR A.
	BURNS A.J.		DICK R.
	BURTON R.F.		DICKINSON G.
	BYRON J.		DICKINSON R.
	CAMERON A.		DICKSON J.R.
	CAMERON J.H.		DIMMICK S.
	CAMPBELL A.		DINHAM F.
	CAMPBELL J.		DOLAN J.
	CANTON J.		DONALD B.S.
	CARE J.		DONALD D.
	CARNEGIE D.L.		DONOGHUE J.
	CARNEY J.J.		DOWLING W.
	CARR E.F.		DRISCOLL M.
	CASS A.		DUFF J.

Pte.	DUNCAN H. St.C.	Pte.	HALL J.H.
	DUNCAN J.G.		HALL J.J.
	DUNCAN J.M.		HALL V.
	DUNCANSON G.		HALLEY A.
	DUNLOP W.A.		HALLMARK E.H.
	DURIE W.		HALLSON A.
	DUTTON S.B.		HANLON J.
	EASTERMAN J.		HARDY J.W.
	EATWELL W.		HARDY S.
	ELLINGSON M.		HARGREAVES R.
	ENGELBRECHT P.A.		HARKNESS J.A.
	EVANS E.R.		HARLEY J.B.
	EVANS G. (259)		HARRINGTON E.W.
	EVANS G. (307)		HARRIS W.D.
	EVANS W.		HARRISON R.
	EVERETT R.C.		HAY R.
	FAIRLESS G.K.		HAYWARD W.C.
	FARLEY J.P.		HEALY B.J.
	FARRELLY J.		HEAP H.
	FERRIE A.E.		HEARSAY G.W.
	FINN W.		HEATH W.
	FISHER S.		HEAWOOD J.
	FITZPATRICK B.J.		HEDDON W.J.
	FLYNN J.		HENDERSON J.
	FOLEY J.		HENDERSON W.M.
	FORBES A.		HENLEY H.
	FOOTE A.		HENRY J.
	FORD A.S.		HEYDENRYCH R.G.
	FORGE T.		HIGGINS A.D.
	FORREST J.		HIGGINS H.
	FOTHERGILL R.		HIGGINS P.
	FOWLES E.W.		HIGGINS W.C.
	FOX T.		HILL H.
	FRASER J.		HILTON J.
	FREY R.		HOLLAND H.E.
	FROST E.		HOLLAND W.G.
	FULLER V.C.		HOLLANDER B.
	GARDNER H.		HOLLIS W.D.
	GARRITY T.		HORROCKS C.
	GARVIE W.J.		HOSKINS C.
	GEER T.K.		HOWARD P.
	GEMMELL A.		HOWARD W.T.
	GIFKINS A.J.		HOY W.J.
	GILBERT G.		HUNT J.R.
	GILBERT W.		HUNTER N.
	GILL A.		HURLEY J.
	GILLARD C.K.		HURLEY T.C.
	GILMOUR R.		HUTCHESON J.
	GOLDWASSER M.		HUTCHINGS N.
	GOODWIN G.E.		HUTCHISON D.
	GORMLEY B.		HUTCHISON G.A.
	GORRY J.		IRVING F.
	GOUGH J.C.		IRWIN C.
	GOURLAY D.B.		IRWIN J.R.
	GRADIDGE H.M.		ISENBERG L.
	GRAHAM D.		IZETT H.
	GRAY A.		JACK F.
	GREEN E.		JACKMAN W.
	GREEN E.E.		JACKSON G.M.
	GREEN R.		JACKSON J.
	GREEN W.		JACKSON R.
	GREER T.K.		JACOBS T.H.
	GREIG J.		JAMES F.C.
	GREIG R.		JAMES T.S.
	GREY H.		JELLIE J.
	GRIFFITHS G.M.		JENKINS J.
	GRIFFITHS W.		JOHNSON C.
	GUMALIUS F.A.		JOHNSTONE F.T.A.
	GUNTER O.		JOHNSTONE J.E.
	HADDEN H.		JOHNSTONE W.J.
	HAIGH B.		JONES G.
	HAILSTONES F.		JONES J. (70)

Pte.	JONES J. (228)		Pte.	McFARLANE G.

Pte.   JONES J. (228)
        JONES J.W.
        JORDAN J.
        JOUBERT I.J.
        KAY J.
        KEIDIAN M.
        KEITH S.
        KELLY C.
        KELLY H.E.
        KELLY J.
        KENNEDY J.
        KENNON S.
        KERMANE L.A.
        KERR W.F.
        KERSHAW H.
        KIPPENDALE J.
        KIRKWOOD D.G.
        KNIGHT S.H.
        KRUGER G.H.
        LAING D. (56)
        LAING D. (219)
        LAMBERT H.
        LAVERY J.
        LAWLESS L.
        LAWRENCE R.
        LAX B.
        LEDLIE J.
        LEE A.E.
        LEES F.W.
        LEITCH S.R.
        LEVY L.B.
        LIGHTFOOT A.G.
        LINDLEY S.T.
        LIPMANN H.
        LITTLETON E.R.
        LOGUE J.S.
        LOWRY R.
        LUMSDEN R.M.
        LYNCH J.
        MACAULEY E.
        MacDONALD D.
        MacDONALD J.
        MACKENZIE W.F.
        MacNAB M.G.
        MACKINTOSH J.
        MacPHERSON J.
        MAHERRY J.J.
        MAITLAND J.S.
        MALLOY P.
        MAPLE W.J.
        MARONEY M.
        MARONEY T.
        MARRIOTT J.S.
        MARSHALL J.
        MARTIN W.
        MASSEY J.
        MATHESON W.L.
        McALLISTER A.
        McALPINE C.
        McBEAN A.
        McBETH A.
        McCALL J.J.
        McCALL T.
        McCOOK J.
        McDONALD A.
        McDONALD C.
        McDONALD J.
        McDONNELL V.
        McDOWALL J.
        McELMINNEY J.
        McEWAN A.

Pte.   McFARLANE G.
        McFARLANE J. (112)
        McFARLANE J. (445)
        McGARRY H.
        McGEE D.C.
        McGRATH T.
        McGREAL M.H.
        McILLWAINE W.R.
        McINNES A.
        McKAY T.J.
        McKAY W.
        McKENNA J.
        McKENZIE A.D.
        McKENZIE D.
        McKINZIE R.
        McKINLEY T.
        McLAREN D.
        McLAUGHLIN F.
        McLEAN S.
        McLEAN W.
        McMAHON R.H.
        McMULLEN P.
        McNAB A.
        McNAIR A.
        McPHERSON J.
        McPHILLANEY T.
        McRAE J.
        McSWEENY P.
        MEEGAN T.
        MELIA J.
        MIKKELSTON A.
        MILL D.
        MILLER J.
        MINTY J.
        MISSING H.W.
        MITCHELL D.
        MITCHELL F.M.
        MOIR W.
        MONTEATH H.
        MOONEY W.R.
        MOORE A.H.
        MOORE T.
        MORE G.
        MORGAN F.
        MORGAN W.
        MORRISON J.
        MORRISON J.H.
        MORRISON W.
        MORTIMER C.
        MORTON J.W.
        MUIR W.
        MULLANEY T.
        MULMERN P.
        MUNDY B.
        MUNRO H.T.
        MUNRO N.A.S.
        MURRAY G.L.
        MURRAY H.J.
        MURRAY P.
        MURROW P.
        MUSGRAVE J.W.
        NEILSON C.
        NETTA O.
        NEVILLE J.F.
        NEWMAN W.F.
        NICKEL B.
        NICHOLAS R.G.
        NICHOLL T.
        NICOL J.D.
        NILSEN M.G.
        O'BRIEN W.

Pte.	O'CONNOR J.V.P.	Pte.	SEELY H.A.
	O'DONNELL G.		SEXTON W.
	OGSTONE R.		SHARP J.H.
	OLIVIER A.G.		SHAW W.A.
	O'REILLY M.T.		SHIELDS F.
	ORTON P.E.		SIMS R.
	PAGE J.W.C.		SIMPSON R.
	PARK J.		SIMPSON R.D.
	PARK J.S.		SINCLAIR J.
	PASSMORE A.C.		SINGLETON J.
	PATRICK J.		SLABBERT J.
	PATTERSON D.		SMITH A. (185)
	PAXTON A.L.		SMITH A. (324)
	PAYNE W.J.		SMITH A.C.
	PEET W.		SMITH G.
	PENNEFATHER V.		SMITH J.
	PHILLIPS H.		SMITH W.
	PHILLIPS J.		SMYTH W.
	PICKARD T.A.		SOULSBY R.
	PILBROW H.J.		SPENCER E.
	PINCH J.J.		SPINKS W.K.
	PINNICK F.W.		SPRIGGS H.J.
	PINNICK G.H.		STATON S.A.
	POLLOCK E.J.T.		STAUNTON P.F.
	POOLE H.G.		STEAD G.H.
	POTHECARY G.		STEVENSON D. (403)
	POVEY C.		STEVENSON D. (411)
	PRAED G.H.		STEVENSON R.
	PRESTON T.		STEWART J.A.
	PRICE J.P.		STEWART R.M.
	PRICE T.M.		STIER G.P.
	PRIEST J.		STONE A.D.
	PRINGLE H.		STONE S.
	PRYCE P.W.		STOREY M.
	PULLOCK A.C.		STOTT W.
	PURDON G.R.		STRACHAN J.
	PURVIS W.		STUART J.
	QUIRK M.		SUTHERLAND T.
	QUIRK T.		SUTTON F.
	RAMSAY W.B.		SWEENY J.C.
	RANGER H.B.		TABATEAU H.
	RAVEN H.E.J.		TATE A.R.
	RAYFIELD J.		TAYLOR H.O.
	REED A.E.		TAYLOR J. (209)
	REED H.A.		TAYLOR J. (303)
	REYNOLDS H.W.		TAYLOR M.
	RICHARDSON T.W.		TENBY E.
	RIDGARD H.H.		THOMPSON A.
	RITSON W.		THOMPSON C.A.
	ROBERTS J.		THOMPSON T.
	ROBERTS L.W.		THOMPSON W.R.
	ROBERTS W.S.		THOMS J.C.
	ROBERTSON J.		THURGOOD R.R.
	ROBERTSON W.M.		THURSBY W.
	ROBINSON F.		TODD W.
	ROLAND G.F.		TOMS W.J.
	ROLT F.J.		TOOMS T.
	ROPER C.W.		TOWNSHEND J.H.
	ROSS W.		TUCKER E.S.
	ROTHWELL J.		TURNBULL A.
	ROWBOTHAM W.H.		TURNBULL J.
	ROWE J.F.W.		TURNER W.
	RUDDOCK B.		TWEEDIE T.
	RUTTER R.S.		TYNAN M.
	RYDER G.		UTTERTON J.
	SAMMONS T.		VAIL J.
	SAUNDERS J.		VAN DER SCHYFF P.
	SCHABRAM A.		VAN BLERK W.S.
	SCOTT J. (206)		VEEVERS A.
	SCOTT J. (382)		VENTER H.
	SEABY T.		VERGETTE R.S.
	SEAGER G.		VINCENT J.

Pte.	VON GUTTENBERG L.V.		Pte.	BROOM W.
	WADDELL T.			CANVIN C.
	WADDEN R.			CARR C.W.
	WALKER C.			CHAPMAN P.
	WALKER F.			CLUNIE J.
	WALKER R.			COLLINS E.T.
	WALKER W.			CUNNINGHAM T.
	WALLIS R.E.			CURRAN J.
	WALSH G.A.			DARLOW H.J.
	WALSH J.			DAVIS C.C.
	WALSH J.F.			DAVIS J.W.
	WALSH T.E.			EDWARDS T.
	WARREN G.			ELSTEAD W.P.C.
	WARING O.L.			ELY F.G.
	WATSON G.			GIDNEY W.M.
	WATSON J. (381)			GILLIT A.E.
	WATSON J. (389)			HOLT A.G.
	WATSON W.			HUTCHINSON E.
	WEBB W.H.			JENKINS D.
	WEBSTER J.R.			JENKIN D.A.
	WHEELER C.			JEWELL B.W.
	WHITE C.W.			JOHNSTONE T.
	WHITE E.E.			JORGENSEN A.E.
	WHITE S.T.			KIBBLEWHITE C.
	WHITEHOUSE R.			KILGOUR J.
	WHITEWRIGHT W.			KIPPS F.C.
	WHITMAN T.W.			KIRKLAND H.C.
	WHITTICK J.			KIRKPATRICK K.
	WHITWORTH M.			LAKING W.
	WHYTE J.			LAWFORD W.A.
	WILES H.			LEWIS R.
	WILLIAMS A.V.			LOFTHOUSE H.
	WILLIAMS C.J.			McDONALD A.
	WILLIAMS S.			McEVOY J.
	WILLIAMSON J.A.			McKENZIE W.
	WILLMOT J.			McLACHLAN J.
	WILLS W.			NEAL G.H.
	WILSON J. (366)			NEWBURY A.W.
	WILSON J. (446)			PALMER D.A.
	WILSON T.A.			PARR H.G.
	WINGER J.			PAYNE E.
	WOOD F.			REEVES J.
	WOOD H.			ROBERTSON P.
	WOOD W.			RULE J.H.
	WOODS H.			SLATER H.H.
	WOODS J.			SMITH J.N.
	WOOD W.H.			SMITH L.N.
	WOODHOUSE J.			SOUTTER S.
	WOODLAND E.H.			STEBBING J.E.
	WOODMANS C.			STEWART D.J.
	WOODWARD B.H.			STOREY H.E.
	WOOLEY P.J.			SWEENEY J.
	WOOSTER H.			THOMPSON W.A.
	WORSLEY L.F.			TUCKETT C.H.
	WRIGHT E.J.			WANTON E.B.
	WRIGHT M.W.			WEBSTOCK H.O.
	WRIGHT W.H.			WHITE J.N.
	YARBERTY W.			WILLIAMS F.
	YOUNG C.F.			WILSON J.
	YOUNG R.			WOOD J.

No Clasps Issued

Sgt. LISTER H.
Cpl. GELL J.H.H.
Pte. ALLEN A.
 ALLEY W.T.
 APEL L.H.T.
 BAXTER J.
 BENARES L.L.
 BRITTAIN F.H.

Total of 907 Awards

With Clasps - 839

No Clasps - 68

Died on Service - Pte. A. McInnes - 8.7.06

NATAL ROYAL REGIMENT
With Clasp 1906
Roll No. 3

Maj.	CAPSTICK H.B.	Pte.	BASTERFIELD G.
	FRASER J.		BELL W.
	LABISTOUR G.A. de R.		BELL W.A.
			BINDON W.E.
Capt.	ASH H.T.		BLAKE G.
	MACKENZIE A.		BLANN C.S.
	RAYMOND G.H.B.		BOLTON L.
Lt.	COLLINS E.		BORLAND J.M.
	COOPER A.R.C.		BOWDEN P.H.J.
	TYRRELL E.G.H.		BRASCH E.
			BRUCE D.
S/M	OGDEN T.C.		BRYSON J.
B/Mast.	BATEMAN B.		CAMERON J.
QMS	CHENEY W.S.		CARBUTT C.F.
Col/Sgt.	DEVERNEUIL F.G.		CASS J.
	DUANE G.S.		CAVANAGH J.
	HOWARD J.C.		CHATHAM M.
	LIGHTFOOT T.		CHILDS A.
	WEATHERDON A.R.		CHITTOCK H.
			CLARK W.
ORS	WALTERS W.H.		COLE G.C.
Sgt.	BAINES J.R.		COLLARD H.
	BANES H.E.		COLLARD J.W.
	BREMMER J.		COOMBES H.D.
	BRESLER V.T.		COTTRELL T.
	BURRINGTON-HAM H.W.		CRONK W.E.
	CARVER G.		CROUCH J.A.
	GLADWIN O.		CUMMINGS J.F.
	HARPER J.		DALEY J.
	HENDERSON W.		DAWSON T.
	LINDSAY E.L.		DEANE E.S.
	POISSON P.E.M.		DENTON G.
	THOMSON J.		DONKIN F.W.
	WALKER W.J.		DUIGAN J.
	WHEELER J.		DUNN R.F.
Cpl.	BARKER R.D.		EATON H.F.
	BINKS F.L.		ELKINGTON E.
	BREWER J.H.		ELKINGTON E.C.
	CRACE T.L.		ELSWORTH A.
	CRERAR A.		EMANUEL L.
	EDMONDS C.A.G.		EVANS J.
	FORBES H.S.		FAULKNER H.
	HARTLEY A.		FLANDERS W.E.
	HOBDAY A.W.		FLEMING J.
	HODNETT W.G.		FOX W.
	HOLLIDAY H.		FRIEND R.
	MARTIN A.C.		FROW H.
	PLATT F.L.		FRYER A.E.
	RHODES S.R.		GAUNT C.W.
	SMITH L.		GOODWIN J.
	UPFOLD T.		GOYARD H.
	WARNER J.W.		GRANT W.
	WOODLEY W.H.		GREEN W.J.A.
Dmr.	BREWER W.R.		GRIFFITHS G.
	CRERAR T.		GUTRIDGE H.
	FIGG D.		HALLEY W.
	HORN J.W.		HARRIS J.A.
	JAMES A.E.		HARRISON A.E.
	JAMES C.		HAWORTH J.M.
	JAMES E.A.		HAY D.R.
	LINFORTH E.A.		HENNESSEY E.J.A.
	LOW A.A.		HERITAGE W.
	MACK W.H.		HESKETH A.W.
	PULLOCK J.		HILL F.
	STRANACK E.T.		HODNETT B.H.
	WHEELER C.S.		HOPKINS C.E.
	WHITHERSPOON R.		HULL H.K.
	WORLAND F.		HUMPHREY F.
Pte.	ADENDORFF H.J.C.		HUNT S.
	ALWICK J.		HUTCHISON W.
	BAKEWELL C.H.		JACKSON J.
			JAMES A.W.

Pte.	JAMES J.		Pte.	VON BERG A.
	JAMES P.R.			VON BERG B.
	JORDAN O.			WALTERS C.E.
	JOY G.H.B.			WARD C.J.
	KANE J.			WATERMAN G.W.
	KEITH K.J.			WATERMAN H.R.
	KELLY P.			WEBSTER G.E.
	KEMP H.			WEBSTER P.V.
	LANE E.			WELDON C.J.
	LAWSON L.			WELDON H.
	LEONARD E.W.			WICKENS H.
	LEONARD J.H.			WINTERBOER W.
	LEWIS C.			WRIGHT G.
	LOXLEY H.			YORK B.

Pte.
- JAMES J.
- JAMES P.R.
- JORDAN O.
- JOY G.H.B.
- KANE J.
- KEITH K.J.
- KELLY P.
- KEMP H.
- LANE E.
- LAWSON L.
- LEONARD E.W.
- LEONARD J.H.
- LEWIS C.
- LOXLEY H.
- MARR A.J.
- MARR W.P.
- MARTIN S de W
- MAY F.
- McGREGOR D.
- McINTOSH W.
- McINTYRE D.W.
- McKEOWN B.
- McKEOWN E.L.
- McNEILL D.
- MEYER C.W.E.
- MITCHELL D.
- MITCHELL W.S.
- MORRISSEY W.
- NAISMITH D.
- NEL G.
- NICHOLSON A.C.
- ONGLEY T de S.W.
- PAGE E.
- PALMER E.J.
- PATERSON A.
- PENDOCK H.F.
- PERFECT A.
- PERFECT S.N.
- POLLARD H.
- POLLARD J.
- PRATT W.H.
- PURVES J.A.
- RAW H.E.
- REARDON P.J.C.
- RICHARDS J.G.
- RIGBY S.
- ROSS R.
- ROWELL F.J.
- ROWLES W.B.
- ROXBURGH H.G.
- SIBTHORP A.E.
- SMITH S.
- SPOONER E.V.
- STEWART C.
- STOCKWELL R.
- STORRIER W.W.
- STRONGMAN J.W.
- TAYLOR A.S.
- TAYLOR E.G.
- THOMPSON W.H.
- THORPE H.D.
- TILEY H.
- TILEY J.
- TODD L.W.
- TURNELL R.
- TWEEDDALE A.M.
- UPFOLD J.H.
- UPPINK J.F.
- VAN BLERCK A.
- VAN RENSBURG M.L.
- VENTER N.

Pte.
- VON BERG A.
- VON BERG B.
- WALTERS C.E.
- WARD C.J.
- WATERMAN G.W.
- WATERMAN H.R.
- WEBSTER G.E.
- WEBSTER P.V.
- WELDON C.J.
- WELDON H.
- WICKENS H.
- WINTERBOER W.
- WRIGHT G.
- YORK B.

No Clasps Issued

Lt/Col.	MATTERSON A.W.
Lt.	KUFAL A.O.
Lt/Qm.	MACKENZIE W.J.M.
Sgt.Ck.	ANSELL J.E.
Sgt.Drum.	ALCOCK G.T.
Sgt.	ANDERSON G.R.
	RUNCIE J.
Cpl.	CLEWLOW R.D.
	COUZENS J.C.
	MORRELL E.B.
Dmr.	FRASER D.A.
	POACHER J.
	ROBERTSON W.T.
Pte.	ADENDORFF H.J.C.
	BAILEY J.G.
	BARKER J.
	BASSETT W.
	BORLAND A.S.
	BOYES C.E.
	BROWN J.M.
	GILLON J.
	GODDARD J.H.W.
	JOHNSON W.
	KNOWLES J.H.
	LANG A.
	LOOSE J.W.
	PURDY C.E.
	REIM A.
	SMITH H.
	SYMES J.R.
	TAYLOR F.R.W.
	UPPINK F.
	WINDSOR H.

Total of 258 Awards

With Clasps - 225

No Clasps - 33

NATAL SERVICE CORPS.
With Clasp 1906
Roll No. 8

Capt.	BOUSFIELD A.
	PRIOR A.
	SMITH F.
Lt.	BRACE E.
	STEWART L.D.
2nd Lt.	CARTER H.B.
	ROHRS E.E.H.
	SMITH H.C.
	WILLS D.W.

RQMS	TARRANT A.E.
QMS	KING E.G.
S/Sgt.	BUTCHER I.A. MSM
	MARSHALL E.W.
	WILLOUGHBY T.B.
Sgt.	BOYD J.E.
	COBB C.
	DAVIDSON J.A.A.
	DAVIES D.
	DIXON R.F.
	LAKE J.B.
	NIBLETT J.A.
	PITTAM T.
	SIMPSON J.T.
	SMITH H.Y.
	WINTER J.
Cpl.	ALLEY G.F.
	BARKER W.H.
	BLACKMORE A.
	GAWNE J.R.
	GILBERT R.F.
	GLASSCOCK W.R.
	GREGORY G.I.
	HARESNAPE W.
	JAMES D.
	NEWSON E.G.
	NORTON H.S.
	RHODES W.B.
	SCARLETT J.S.
	SIMMONS C.W.
Tpr.	ABBOTT C.E.
	ALLANSON A.B.
	ANDERSON J.G.
	BALLENDEN F.B.
	BARKLEY P.
	BEVERSTOCK A.
	BOUTTELL F.
	BRUIN E.C.
	BURTON B.W.
	CLARKE J.O.
	COX J.G.
	CROWTHER A.
	DALZELL J.
	DALZELL T.
	DANBY G.E.
	DEWAR W.J.
	DUNLOP D.
	ELLCOCK S.E.
	FISHER B.
	FORD T.K.
	GIBSON F.G.
	GIBSON G.
	GILLESPIE J.
	GLASS J.F.
	GORDON E.T.
	GRIX R.L.
	GRUNDY S.H.
	HARRISON F.H.
	HARRISON L.V.
	HAWORTH R.W.B.
	HOLMES E.H.
	HOSKINS A.
	HYSLOP J.E.
	JESSUP G.J.
	JONES J.
	KENNA L.G.
	LONGLEY W.
	LORRIMER J.H.
	MALCOLM J.
	MANSON S.
	MAXWELL R.M.
Tpr.	McDONALD J.
	McDONALD R.
	McDONALD W.H.
	MILNE A.P.
	MOCKLER J.
	MORLING R.F.
	MUNRO D.
	MURPHY A.T.
	NELSON F.
	NICKERSON H.
	NOONAN D.
	NYBERG I.
	OAKLEY D.D.
	PEACOCK G.H.
	PERCY A.
	PEYTO A.G.
	PHILLIP E.
	PITTAM J.
	POPE F.J.
	RAFTER F.
	REAY J.A.
	RUSHTON P.
	SAXBY H.H.
	SIMPSON F.H.
	STURGEON F.O.
	SUTHERLAND W.A.
	THOMPSON G.
	TREVOR W.
	WHITESIDE N.R.
	WILKINSON E.E.
	WILSON A.

No Clasps Issued

Sgt.	WILLIAMS F.C.
Cpl.	SMITH J.
Tpr.	CAMP E.
	FINNING F.W.
	FRIEND A.J.
	MORGAN A.
	WATT W.B.
	WICK J.

Total of 119 Awards

With Clasps - 111

No Clasps - 8

Note; The handwriting on the roll was rather difficult to read and so some of the I's and J's may be mistaken for the other.

NATAL TELEGRAPH CORPS.
With Clasp 1906
Roll No. 9

Capt.	FRASER F.
Lt.	ANDERSON R.S.
QMS	FOSTER F.A.
Sgt.	BURTON J.C.
	POWELL W.
L/Sgt.	EASTON R.A.
	JEANES A.J.
Cpl.	CRAWFORD J.F. MSM
	DUNNING C.
	FERRIS C.
	HANCOX S.
Tpr.	BAYLIS B.C.
	BLAKE R.H.

Tpr.	BULKLEY H.W.T.
	CAMERON D.A.
	CLARK W.J.A.
	DUNNING H.J.
	FEARN E.F.
	FLACK B. V H.
	FORBES D.C.
	FURZE F.W.
	HALL J.C.
	HEX S.P.
	KELLAWAY A.G.
	MARTIN H.
	McDONALD T.
	MEDHURST F.W.
	MILLS W.R.
	NOBLE W.
	PAUL A.
	PEMBERTON J.F. MSM
	PERKINS W.J.
	POOLE R.R.
	RAYNER F.G.
	REA A.
	SALMON D.A.
	TEAGUE P.W.
	THORP R.

No Clasps Issued

QMS	FOSTER A.R.
Sgt.	CRADDOCK F.A.
	FERGUSON G.
Tpr.	BOOTH J.
	ROUSE J.B.
	WALKER J.W.

Total of 44 Awards

With Clasps - 38

No Clasps - 6

NATAL VETERINARY CORPS.
With Clasp 1906
Roll No. 11

Maj.	WOOLATT S.B.
Capt/Adj.	AMOS S.T.
Capt.	CORDY C.H.
	O'NEILL O.A.
	POWER W.M.
	SHARPE C.M.
	TYLER C.
Lt.QM.	HIME M.J.
QMS	BROWN A.
Sgt.	BOWLES E.W.
Tpr.	PURDY W.

No Clasps Issued

Capt.	HARBER A.F.
	OLIVER H.O.

Total of 13 Awards

With Clasps - 11

No Clasps - 2

NEWCASTLE DIVISION RESERVES
No Clasps Issued
Roll No. 51

Chief Leader	ADENDORFF M.C.
Leader	WATSON C.
Sub.Ldr.	DEWET C.L.
	MULLER A.M.
Sgt.Maj.	WATSON J.L.
QMS	McKIE T.
Sgt.	LUCAS A.W.
Cpl.	COENRADIE W.
	CRONJE G.L.
	DEGENAAR A.
	DONOVAN E.L.
	FOURIE K.P.
	GODWIN R.
	JONES M.
	STEPHANS R.
	TAYLOR J.E.
	WYLIE B.D.
Tpr.	ACKERMAN J.
	ADENDORFF D.
	ADENDORFF F.
	ANDERSON F.W.
	BARKER A.G.
	BOSHOFF J.
	BOSHOFF J.
	BOSHOFF W.H.
	BOTHA B.
	BOWMAN
	BROOKES
	COENRADIE P.
	CRONJE C.
	CRONJE J.
	CRONGE W.
	DANNHAUSER J.A.
	De BRUIN H.
	DEGENAAR L.
	DELPORT A.C.
	DENNELL A.C.
	De VILLIERS C.J.
	De WET D.R.
	De WET P.W.
	DIMOCK R.
	DOUBELL G.
	ELKER C.
	EKSTEIN G.
	GRANT A.
	GREAVES R.H.
	HUMAN J.
	JONKER A.
	JORDAAN G.D.
	JORDAAN N.P.
	JOUBERT J.
	KELLY M.
	KLOPPER J.
	KOCH D.J.
	MARAIS A.
	MARAIS J.
	MARSHALL A.S.
	MATTHEWS G.
	McDONALD J.
	MEYER H.
	MORRIS J.A.C.
	MOSS C.
	NIEUWINHUYSEN Z.
	O'NEIL H.

Tpr.	OOSTHUYSEN N.		Tpr.	FORTMANN H.C.H.
	O'REILLY J.R.			FORTMANN H.W.
	OSBORNE W.			FORTMANN J.W.
	PRINSLOO P.			FORTMANN O.
	RALL S.			FREESE F.H.A.
	RATHBORN E.			FREESE G.C.W.
	REDMAN D.			FREESE H.J.
	REDMAN G.			HABERMANN C.
	REDMAN W.			HOHLS C.H.A.
	SCHNELL C.			HOHLS E.G.C.
	SCHWIKKARD A.V.			HOHLS H.F.W.
	SCHWIKKARD B.			HOLLEY W.C.
	SWAARTS J.S.			KLIPP G.
	SWAMERS A.J.			KOCH J.
	SYMONS B.			KONING J.
	TEASDALE F.			LAMBSCH R.
	THOMAS H.E.			LUCHT G.
	THOMAS W.G.			LUNENBURG F.A.
	UYS P.			LUNENBURG J.H.F.
	VAN NIEKERK M.C.			MAKKINK F.
	WATT C.J.			MEIERHOF W.
	WOOD J.M.			MEYER C.
	ZIETSMAN J.			MUMMBRAUER H.
	ZIETSMAN M.H.			OELLERMANN D.G.L.
				OELLERMANN G.

Total of 88 Awards

With Clasp - Nil

No Clasps - 88

NEW HANOVER RESERVES
No Clasps Issued
Roll No. 50

Chief				OELLERMANN G.H.W.
Leader	EHLERS H.H.W.			OELLERMANN H.C.
Leader	HOHLS J.H.F.			OELLERMANN G.H.
Sub.Lead.	ELLING J. VON			OELLERMANN H.F.O.
	SMITH M.M.			OELLERMANN O.L.
	SOLOMON O.M.			OELLERMANN S.A.F.
RSM	DODD G.F.			PAUL F.
QMS	DALE J.W.			PENTLAND H.
Sgt.	FORTMANN H.F.C.			ROEHRS F.
	RODEHORST C.			ROSENBROCK H.J.
	SCHALLENBERG H.W.F.			SCOTT C.M.
OR.Cpl.	SCHULZE F.J.			THOELE C.H.F.
Cpl.	DICKENS A.			THOELE F.C.B.
	DICKENS C.J.			VORWERK E.F.W.
	HABERMANN H.			WILSON L.
	HILLERMANN W.			WITTIG E.R.
	JACKSON M.			WOLHUTER G.F.J.
	MEYER P.			
	OELLERMANN C.W.H.		Total of 75 Awards	
	OELLERMANN R.J.P.			
	PECKHAM S.		With Clasps - Nil	
	RODEHORST J.			
Tpr.	ALLWOOD G.F.		No Clasps - 75	
	BOSSE A.			
	BOSSE H.			
	BOSSE W.		**NKANDHLA TOWN GUARD**	
	BUNN J.R.		No Clasps Issued	
	COMINS C.C.		Roll No. 59	
	CULVERWELL C.J.			
	EGGERS C.		No Rank	BREW W.C.
	EGGERS H.F.W.			COOPER T.W.
	ELS P.			DICKSON W.H.
	FINTEL H. VON			DOUGLAS A.E.
	FORTMANN B.			FORDER F.W.
				FRY H.
				GODFREY T.W.
				HYSLOP C.R.L.
				KENNEDY J.
				MAN H.C.H.
				McKENZIE G.
				MOORE A.
				RITCHIE W.
				SCHREIBER O.
				STANDAGE T.
				TURNER H.

No Rank   WOTTOW T.

Total of 17 Awards

With Clasps - Nil

No Clasps   - 17

Note: To these names could have been added that of Revd. L.E. Oscroft - Nkandhla Town Guard, who is listed with the Chaplains.

NORTHERN DISTRICTS MOUNTED RIFLES
With Clasp 1906
Roll No. 28

Maj.	ABRAHAM J.
Capt.	DE WAAL G.M.
	ENTE J.S.
	WILKINS H.
Capt/Adj.	HOWARD L.M.
Hon.Lt/QM.	RAND C.
Lt.	ABRAHAM J.A.
	DEWAR R.
	IRELAND W.J.
	LLOYD R.
	MacKENZIE S.S.
	PFAFF D. Mc. L.M.
	RUNDLE F.S.
	SUTER R.A.
RSM	AUSTIN W.P.
RQMS	BOYD J.L.
SSM	BRIANT A.F.
	PERRYMAN W.M.
SQMS	CUMMING J.
	HACKLAND J.
	VINCER R.A.
OR.Sgt.	BAILEY W.
Sgt.Sad.	PAGE J.
Sgt.Tail.	CHISHOLM D.
Far.Sgt.	EVANS J.
Sgt.	BAKER S.
	BARR W.F.
	BEATTIE J.W.
	CURLE J.H.
	CURTIS T.J.B.
	LINDER J.B.
	MASON J.A.
	NEL A.H.
	NEL G.
	ROBERTS E.J.
	RUSSOUW E.
	SANDERSON A.F.
	STACKWOOD W.
	SWATTON P.G.
Cpl.S.S.	WILLIAMS E.J.
Cpl.	ANGUS A. Mc.F.
	BEATER E.R.
	BOTHA H.S.
	COMBRINK L.M.
	DA HAAS T.H.
	DOUGLASS W.
	DYER J.H.
	ELLIS T.J.
	GOULD G.E.W.
	HARDIE J.
	HAY D.
	HOWARD P.
	KRUGER G.
	LEWARNE C.
Cpl.	MASKILL J.T.
	MOSSOP L.B.
	PIETERSE G.C.
	PIETERSE J.F.
	ROBERTS M.J.F.
	SCHWAB J.D.
	SHARPE G.C.
	TATHAM H.E.
	VOLKER C.
	WRIGHT T.
	ZIETSMAN B.H.
Tmptr.	ABRAHAM J.M.
	SCHULTZ O.V.
Tpr.	ABRAHAM A.
	ANDERSON R.
	ARTHURTON W.G.
	BADENHORST G.H.
	BARRY W.J.
	BECK J.G.
	BENNET J.
	BENTLEY T.J.
	BEUKES R.
	BEZUIDENHOUT H.J.
	BEZUIDENHOUT J.J.C.
	BEZUIDENHOUT M.J.F.
	BLACKBURN J.
	BORLICK T.
	BRIGHT T.
	CARLARN D.
	CARMODY P.
	CHALLENOR K.
	CLARK W.
	COETZEE C.J.
	COLEMAN P.
	COOKE T.A.
	CORNELIUS J.P.
	COXELL W.H.
	CUNNINGHAM J.
	DEERE R.
	DEKKAR P.D.
	DE WAAL A.A.K.
	DOWAY H.
	DUBERY A.J.
	DUNN J.J.
	DU PLESSIS C.J.
	DU PLESSIS J.A.
	DU PREEZ D.H.
	DYER H.F.
	DYER H.W.
	EVANS H.F.
	FERGUSON C.S.
	FOURIE J.F.
	FRATER F.
	GLUTZ H.W.
	GREIG M.
	GREYLING B.P.F.
	GROVE D.J.
	GUNTER C.F.
	GUNTER D.C.
	HANSEN A.P.
	HARDER W.
	HARPER H.
	HARPER J.
	HARRIS W.
	HEIN F.
	HEIN G.
	HENDRY J.
	HUMPHREYS F.
	HUTCHESON C le M.
	JESPERSON W.
	JESSOP G.
	JONES T.

Tpr.	KILLIAN J.G.	Tpr.	STANLEY D.
	KITCHEN H.J.		STRAW H.
	KLOPPER H.J.C.		SWATTON O.R.
	KOEKOMOER J.J.		THOMPSON J.
	KRIEL L.J.		TRAVERS G.
	KRUGER W.C.		TSCHIRPIG H.
	LABUSCHAGNE J.A.		TURNBULL D.W.
	LAMBERT W.J.		TURTON A.G.
	LANDSBERG W.J.		UNDERHILL W.C.
	LARSEN C.		VAN DER CRAGHT H.S.
	LARSEN L.W.M.		VAN DER CRAGHT P.R.
	LIEBETRAU H.J.H.		VAN DER HEEVER A.J.
	LINDEQUE P.J.		VAN DER WALT G.J.
	LIVERSAGE H.B.		VAN DER ZANT A.J.
	LOMBARD B.J.		VAN RENSBURG H.J.J.
	LOMBARD J.H.		VAN STADEN A.J.
	LOMBARD J.J.		VAN TONDER A.J.
	LOMBARD S.		VERBECK J.
	MACSHANE F.J.		WAREING R.A.
	MARAIS J.L.		WEBB C.J.
	MAREE J.		WESSELS H.J.
	MARITZ C.F.S.		WHITBREAD J.W.J.
	MARITZ C.J.		WIGGEL E.J.
	McDONALD S.		WIGGEL J.O.
	McINDOE W.F.		WILLIAMS J.
	McKAY W.J.		WILLIAMS M.W.A.
	MENGEL J.H.		WILLIAMS P.H.
	MEYER C.J.		WILLIAMSON C.
	MILLS A.W.		WILSON A.G.
	MILLS G.		WOOLMORE B.I.
	MILLWARD W.		WYLLIE J.
	MOSSOP G.E.		YALLAP E.
	MULLER H.S.A.		YALLAP O.H.
	MULLER W.F.		ZUNKUNFT J.
	MURRAY J.R.		
	MYKLEGAARD B.O.	No Clasps Issued	
	NEL T.J.		
	NELSON J.	Sgt.	CHALLENOR O.S.
	NICOL A.		GLUTZ H.J.S.
	OLIVIER G.		HOWARD R.W.
	OOSTHUYZEN L.		NETTER A.J.
	OWENS D.P.	Tpr.	ROSS R.C.
	PALMER J.C.		SCHONECKE P.H.
	PELSTER J.J.		
	PEROTTI E.	Total of 239 Awards	
	PHELAN E.		
	PIENAAR J.G.	With Clasps - 233	
	PIETERS M.M.C.		
	PIETERS P.J.	No Clasps - 6	
	PIETRESE M.J.C.		
	PLAYER H.C.		
	POTGEITER C.J.A.	**NURSES - CIVILLIAN**	
	POTGEITER M.J.	No Clasps Issued	
	PRETORIUS J.H.	Roll No. 59	
	PRETORIUS N.		
	RATHBONE W.M.	Nurse	GRAY A.
	REDMAN A.G.		HINE L.
	REED C.		LAZARUS B.
	REED J.L.		McKENZIE W.
	RENNIE J.		NORMAN G.M.
	ROBBERTSE J.H.		SYMMOTT A.M.
	ROBERTS J.		SYMMOTT
	ROGERS C.		
	SADLER J.	Total of 7 Awards	
	SADLER T.J.		
	SAUNDERS A.	With Clasps - Nil	
	SHARPE R.R.		
	SHARPE R.W.	No Clasps - 7	
	SIEFF E.		
	SLABBERTS J.J.S.		
	SLABBERTS J.S.		
	SMITH A.		
	SMITH H.H.		

ROYSTONS HORSE
With Clasp 1906
Roll No. 37

Lt.Col.	ROYSTON J.P. CMG DSO	
Maj.	FRASER A.W.	
	KNOTT W.	
	WATT J.R.	
Capt.	BOYLE A.T.S.	
	CLERK E.G.	
	FRADD E.H.	
	GODSON G.G.	
	GUNNINGHAM W.G.	
	HATCHWELL H.J.E.	
	ORTON W.F.	
	OSWALD W.D.	
	POLLOCK J.C.	
	THORD-GRAY I.	
	THORPE C.	
Lt.	BLACKBURNE C.C.	
	CADDELL W.W.	
	DAVIS O.	
	FRENCH E.G.F.	
	FRYER T.C.	
	GREAVES G.M.	
	GREEN A.	
	GREEN W.A.G. Esdaile	
	HOPKINS W.H.	
	HUGHES E. St.G.	
	JONES H.R.	
	KENNEDY A.E.	
	MALE P.	
	MARSDEN C.G.	
	McKENZIE R.D.	
	MIDGELEY S.	
	MILLER L.W.	
	MUNRO J.R.	
	PAIN N.F.H.	
	RENTON H.H.	
	SHEEHAN M.R.	
	SHEPSTONE G.H.	
	STEWART C.M.	
	THOMPSON A.	
	WALSHE H.P.	
RSM	WEBBER J. MSM	
RQMS	BROPHY W.	
	CHEADLE F.	
FQMS	HAMILTON H.R.	
SSM	BARLOW J.A.	
	CLARK J.	
	FRASER H.	
	GAVSHON J.	
	HARDIE J.S.	
	LEAN E.A.	
	LIVESAY C.	
	NEWTON J.H.	
	SANDY L.	
	WEBSTOCK H.O.	
ORS	BAILEY W.W.	
	BASSETT J.C.O.	
	MOLYNEUX J.H.	
SQMS	ALEXANDER J.H.	
	BROWNE K.N.	
	GOODWIN G.T.	
	MAJOR L.B.	
	PALLISTER J.	
	PETZOLD E.L.	
	PICK A.J.	
	SWATRIDGE A.	
Arm/Sgt.	SWEENEY J.C.	
Sgt.Cook	HERBERT G.S.	
Farr/Sgt.	BAIN J.	
	BAIN W.D.	
	McKENDRICK J.J.	
	O'DONNELL T.	
	O'RILEY J.	
	WELCH W.J.	
Sad/Sgt.	MAGILL J.	
Tpr.Sgt.	GRIEVES L.W.G.	
	SHUTTLEWORTH C.T.	
Trans.Sgt.	GASKELL J.S.	
	ROSS J.	
Sgt.	ARCHER A.	
	BEATH H.	
	BRODRICK L.St.J.	
	CALDWELL D.	
	CRUDDAS N.	
	DAVIES H.M.	
	DICKER W.A.	
	FITZMAURICE H.	
	FLYNN F.	
	FOSTER H.J.	
	FOWLER W.W.	
	GALLOWAY R.	
	HASTINGS K.	
	HEPWORTH D.S.	
	HILTON F.	
	HOLDSTOCK J.	
	IMRIE J.	
	JUDELS E.J.	
	MAIN J.	
	MARRIOTT W.W.	
	MASSON J.H.	
	MAWLEY A.	
	McKENZIE R.	
	McMILLAN G.J.H.	
	MELDRUM W.T.	
	MORAN A.C.	
	RICHES S.	
	ROBERTSON J.E.	
	SELBY A.W.	
	TANNETT G.	
	WARR W.L.	
	WAUGH E.M.	
OR.Cpl.	MAUD H.L.	
Cpl.	ALEXANDER E.	
	ALEXANDER T.	
	ALLAN J.	
	ANDREWS G.T.	
	ASHBY D.	
	AULD J.	
	BARNETT H.D.M.	
	BARTLEY H.	
	BOLLAND L.A.	
	BOLTON J.	
	BOND W.W.	
	BRIGGS A.W.	
	BUCKLAND L.R.	
	BUTTERFIELD N.W.	
	CASEY J.D.	
	CASSIDY F.	
	COUZENS J.C.	
	DOPSON C.A.	
	DUGGAN B.T.	
	GARDNER T.	
	HENSHAW C.S.	
	JACQUES W.L.	
	JANES A.A.	
	JONES A.B.	
	JOHNSON H.B.	
	JOHNSON J.	
	JOHNSTON F.H.	

Cpl.	JOHNSTONE D.	Tpr.	BAWDEN T.H.
	KING C.		BAYNON P.W.
	KIRBY W.		BEECHEY A.E.
	LIMERICK J.St.C.		BENN W.
	LOSSACK A.S.		BENNETT A.
	LOVELL E.		BENNETT J.
	MANN J.		BERRETT W.
	MASTERSON C.W.		BESWICK F.
	McCORMACK J.		BICKNELL D.
	McKENNA E.		BIGGINS J.
	McMAHON P.		BINDON W.E.
	MEIKLE M.E.		BLAMIRE L.W.
	MERRITT W.		BLYTHE J.W.
	MILLER J.		BOLTON E.
	MOORE W.H.		BORAIN J.
	MORRISON W.		BOUCK J.
	MURPHY J.		BOYD R.N.
	NEWBERRY L.		BOYD W.
	NOLAN P.W.		BRADFORD H.M.
	O'BRIEN T.V.		BRADSHAW R.
	POWELL C.J.		BREEN J.J.
	PRESTON E.A.		BRERETON W.L.
	RAMSAY W.W.		BRINCH C.
	REED P.		BROOME H.A.
	RUSSELL C.		BRIDGOOD C.
	SAINSBURY H.		BROWN H.H.
	SHUTTLE M.L.		BROWN W.I.
	SKILTON R.G.		BROWSE M.
	SOMERS L.		BUCHANAN D.
	SOUTHBY R.		BUCKINGHAM R.
	STAPPARD E.A.		BURGESS F.
	SULLIVAN W.		BURKE J.G.
	SWANSON J.P.		BURKE W.L.
	THOMAS J.H.		BURNE A.T.
	VESEY C.		BURNS C.J.
	VICTOR W.J.		BUTTIMER D.J.
	WALTON F.		BUTTON S.
	WEBB C.F.		BYRNE J.
	WOOLNOUGH H.		CALLAGHAN J.
Saddler	CAWLEY J.G.		CAMERON J.
	CROWLEY J.		CAMERON J.D.
	SMITH H.C.		CAMERON W.
SS.	BERGGREN F.		CAMILLERI S.
	DWYER E.		CAMPBELL H.
	DORSE W.G.		CAMPBELL H.
	JOHNSON B.		CAMPBELL P.
	PERRY J.		CARBUTT R.
	YOUNG W.		CARTER A.
Tmptr.	CUNNINGHAM J.		CARTER C.
Tpr.	ABBOTT G.I.		CARTER R.W.
	ADDICOTT J.		CARTMELL E.
	AGNEW J.		CASEY T.
	ALBERTO P.J.		CASTLE F.
	ALDWELL J.		CHAMBERS H.J.
	ALLANBY C.M.		CHAPMAN S.
	AMOS J.H.		CHARTLIER F.J.
	ANDERSON G.		CHESTER W.
	ANDREWS A.E.		CLARK J.S.
	ANDREWS H.B.		CLARKE F.E.W.
	ANSELL H.R.		CLARKE R.T.
	ANTHONY C.		CLEMENTS S.J.
	ARBUCKLE F.J.		CLINCH J.
	ARMSTRONG J.E.		COLE J.
	ASHLEY F.C.		COLES A.
	ATBRIDGE E.		COOK G.H.
	ATTWOOD O.P.L.		COOKE B.
	BAIRD J.		COOPER L.
	BARNETT W.		COTTERILL T.
	BARR T.		COX F.
	BARMSTEIN J.		CRABBE A.H.
	BARNES J.W.		CRAMOND C.
	BATHURST G.		CREASY W.

Tpr.	CREIGHTON W.J.	Tpr.	GRAHAM P.
	CROCOMBE W.		GRAHAM T.
	CROFT J.D.		GREIG W.
	CUNNAH T.		GRIFFITHS J.H.
	CUNNINGHAM A.		GROBLER J.
	DANNAHER C.D.		GROBLER J.A.
	DASHWOOD J.		GROBLER J.G.
	DAVIES A.W.		GROSE T.
	DAVIES J.W.C.		GRUBB F.W.
	DAVIES E.J.		GUNNING G.
	DAVIS I.		GUNNING J.
	DAWLER W.		HAMILTON A.
	DAWSON A.		HAMILTON B.
	DEACON W.		HAMILTON J. (626)
	DEARE H.		HAMILTON J. (633)
	DE BUDE H.		HAMMOND J.
	DE BURGH J.		HANBURY S.S.
	DE LANGE H.S.		HANLON J.
	DESPARD R.		HANNAN E.
	DE VILLIERS J.A.		HANSEN C.
	DICKENS J.		HARDING C.W.D.
	DICKSON W.M.		HARDING J.
	DILLON R.W.		HARDING S.J.
	DIVINE F.O.S.		HARE W.H.
	DIXON R.		HARRIS A.
	DIXON W.		HARRISON H.J.
	DONALD J.		HAWKINS J.
	DOW J.		HENNESSEY E.J.A.
	DOWLING W.J.		HIGGINS W.
	DOWNEY R.		HILL F.
	DUNLEE J.		HILL P.J.M.
	DYOS T.		HILL T.
	EASTON S.		HILL T.R.
	EATON C.O.		HINE W.H.
	EDWARDS D.R.		HODGSON C.F.
	ELGY M.E.		HODNETT H.
	EMMANUEL P.E.		HOEY P.
	ENWRIGHT J.		HOLMES W.C.
	ERIKSON A.		HOPE G.
	EVANS W.G.		HOPKINS S.
	EWART W.R.		HORAN E.
	FARRAR G.		HORSEFIELD W.
	FEELEY G.E.		HORWOOD H. (75)
	FELLOWES E.		HORWOOD H. (319)
	FELTHAM V.J.		HOSEY J.
	FERGUSON H.J.		HOSKING P.E.
	FIELDER F.E.		HOUSTON W.
	FLETCHER T.		HYNES W.J.
	FOLEY F.A.		ILLINGWORTH E.
	FORD H.P.		INGHAM J.H.
	FOSTER F.		INNIS A.
	FRANCIS W.		IRELAND A.
	FREEMAN E.F.		IRELAND H.F.
	FULLER W.C.		JACK D.
	GAMBLE W.R.		JACK J.M.
	GARDNER W.		JAKES S.
	GATE W.F.		JAMIESON G.
	GATONBY G.L.		JENKINS H.
	GEORGE R.		JENKINS T.
	GIBSON F.G.		JOHNSON F.
	GIBSON P.		JOHNSTONE J.W.
	GILMOUR H.		JONES I.B.
	GLADHILL D.		JONES J.A.
	GODSON R.		JONES J.J.
	GOODALL J.		JONES M.
	GOODE H.		JORDAN H.W.
	GOODWIN D.W.		JOSEPH W.R.
	GORDON G.M.		KATZENSTEIN M.
	GORDON J.		KEENE A.C.
	GOSLETT D.		KEHOE R.
	GOULD W.G.		KELVIE J.
	GRACE T.H.		KENNEDY B.

Tpr.	KERSHAW H.	Tpr.	MIDDLETON W.
	KIMMINER V.H.		MILLER D.O.
	KING A.E.		MILLER J.
	KING C.		MILLS R.E.
	KING G.		MITCHELL A.
	KING J.		MOONEY D.M.
	KINT H.K.		MOORE J.F.
	KIRKWOOD C.		MOORE S.G.
	KIRKWOOD J.G.		MORGAN D.
	KOK F.J.		MORGAN J.
	LAMONT W.		MORRIS J.C.
	LAWRENCE J.		MORRIS J.J.
	LEATH G.		MUIR L.S.
	LEDDRA G.		MUNRO A.
	LEE C.		MURDOCK D.F.
	LEGAT F.W.		MURPHY C.
	LE ROUX P.		MURPHY J.
	LESNEY G.W.		MURRAY G. St.G.W.
	LEVETT P.A.		MURRAY D.
	LEWIS R.H.		NAPIER D.
	LIEBENBERG B.		NEL G.
	LISTER A.L.		NELSON S.
	LITTLE J.		NISBET W.L.
	LIVESAY H.		NOLAN J. (627)
	LLOYD S.E.		NOLAN J. (828)
	LOGAN R.		NOWELL J.
	LORD H.		OATES J.A.
	LOWE J.H.		O'BRYEN J.G.P.
	LOXLEY H.		O'CALLAGHAN D.
	LYDIATE A.		O'FARRELL E.J.
	MacIVER J.		O'MORE A.
	MacKAY J.M.		ONUS J.
	MacKENZIE T.		OVERALL E.
	MAIDMENT W.B.		OVERINGTON J.R.
	MAJOR W.H.		OWEN J.
	MALE E.		OWENS F.
	MALE S.J.		PALMER L.
	MALONE T.		PARKER W.
	MARKS E.W.		PATES H.S.
	MARSH B.		PATRICK D.
	MATSON H.B.		PAUL A.
	MAVOR J.		PAWSON E.
	McCABE W.P.		PAYNE W.
	McCALLUM P.		PERRIN G.H.
	McCAMIS J.		PETERSON N.
	McCAULL J.		PETERSON P.
	McDONALD J.		PHILLIPS E.J.
	McELNEA H.J.		PHILPOTT E.
	McELROY J.H.		PHIPPS V.G.
	McEWAN W.M.		PICKARD C.
	McFARLANE R.		PIGGOTT A.
	McGILLBERY D.		PIGOTT A.
	McGLONE J.E.		PINNOCK R.
	McINDOE J.		POLLARD J.
	McINNES M.		POLLOCK T.
	McINTOSH J.H.		POTTER B.
	McIVER J.		POWELL E.
	McKAY W.J.		POWELL W.C.
	McKENDRICK R.		POWER T.
	McKENDRICK T.		PRENTICE J.
	McKENZIE T.		PURVIS J.T.
	McKINLEY J.M.		QUINN D.
	McLEOD A.J.		RAE G.
	McLEOD G.G.		RATCLIFFE T.
	McMANON M.		RAYMOND T.W.
	McMILLAN D.		REECE W.
	McSHEA J.J.		REIDY M.
	MEDEALFE F.		REYNOLDS R.F.
	MEDLICOTT G.H.		RICE T.
	MEREDITH G.		RICHARDSON C.
	MEREDITH J.		RICHARDSON E.H.
	MIDDLETON E.		RICHARDSON J.W.

Tpr.	ROACH A.J.	Tpr.	THORBURN G.E.
	ROBERTS A.		THORNTON E. (207)
	ROBERTS G.F.		THORNTON E. (478)
	ROBERTSON D.		THORNTON G.R.
	ROBERTSON S.I.		THORPE A.E.
	ROBINSON G.		TIPTON H.
	ROBINSON H.		TODD G.T.
	ROBINSON J.L.		TORRANCE W.
	ROBINSON S.		TOWNSHEND E.H.
	ROBINSON W.G.		TRAFFORD C.
	ROCHE H.		TRANSON J.
	ROLAND C.E.		TRAVERS W.P.G.
	ROLAN W.		TRENCH S.H.
	ROPER H.L.		TUNNY J.
	ROY J.		TURNER R.H.S.
	RUDD E.F.		TYLER S.F.
	RUDLAND L.		ULYATE R.R.
	RUDLING A.		UPTON W.M.
	RUSSELL J.N.H.		URQUHART J.
	RYAN J.H.		VAN BLERCK A.
	SALTER S.		VENDERSANDT J.
	SANDY R.A.		VAN RENSBURG M.L.
	SCALLY M.		VENTER N.
	SCOTT C.B.		VICKERS G.H.
	SCOTT F.		VINGOE J.
	SEALE A.		VIVASH C.
	SEYMOUR R.		VIVIAN C.E.
	SHANNON C.H.		VON MENGERSHAUSEN F.K.
	SHARP J.		VOSPER S.
	SHAW B.		WADE V.J.
	SHEFFIELD A.		WALCROFT E.W.
	SHEPHERD J.H.		WALKER C.C.
	SHERIDAN R.B.		WALKINSHAW M.
	SHIELDS J.S.		WALLIS A.
	SHORT J.		WALSH H.P.
	SHUTTE F.E.N.		WALSH J.
	SILVERSIDE G.		WALSH M.G.
	SIM W.		WARBURG M.
	SKINNER C.J.D.		WARD S.
	SLADEN S.		WARWICK F.
	SMITH A.C.		WATERS G.
	SMITH C.S.		WATT J.
	SMITH E.G.H.		WEBB S.R.
	SMITH G.W.		WEBBER R.
	SMITH J. (201)		WELCH W.
	SMITH J. (393)		WELDON L.
	SMITH J. (595)		WEST W.J.
	SMITH J. (777)		WHELPTON H.
	SMITH R.		WICKHAM J.R.
	SMITH R.M.		WILKINSON E.E.
	SMITH W.T.		WILKINSON J.H.
	SMUTTS N.		WILKINSON R.P.
	SPRING H.T.		WILL J.
	STANLEY A.		WILLIAMS G.
	ST. AUSTIN E.P.		WILLIAMS G.T.
	STRECKER F.C.		WILLIAMS M.H.
	STYLES T.W.		WILLIAMS M.M.
	SUTHERLAND W.H.		WILSON A.V.
	SWART D.		WILSON J. (590)
	TANCREED J.		WILSON J. (625)
	TARBUTT H.		WILSON J. (709)
	TATNELL P.		WILSON W.R.
	TAYLOR W.C.		WINTERBOER W.
	TENNANT D.O.		WINTERS J.G.
	THELWELL F.W.		WINTON A.S.
	THOMAS E.P.		WOOD G.H.
	THOMAS J. (104)		WOOD J.H.
	THOMAS J. (808)		WRIGHT A.C.
	THOMAS M.D.		YARDLEY P.
	THOMPSON A.		YEAMAN W.C.
	THOMPSON F.		YOUNG H.T.
	THOMPSON L.		

No Clasps Issued

RQMS	BEHRENS C.H.
SQMS	WOLFERSTAN S.
Sgt.	NORRIS W.
	YOUNG R.S.
Cpl.	GILVRAY D.
	McDONALD M.
Tpr.	BICKHILL A.J.
	BROWN J.W.
	CLARKE J.
	COOMBES C.R.
	COOPER A.J.
	DUNSTER F.
	DU PLESSIS J.P.
	FOLEY J.
	HAMILTON H.J.
	HICKMAN C.H.
	HIRST T.B.
	HOBBS F.
	HORNE B.C.
	KNOTT H.
	HUMPHREY F.
	PITOUT J.W.
	RICHARDS D.
	SHERWOOD W.H.
	SHEVLIN P.
	SHUTTE R.T.
	SMITH J.B.
	WARD J.C.
	WOOD A.E.W.
	WILSON J.C.
	WOOD W.W.

Total of 745 Awards

With Clasps - 714

No Clasps - 31

Killed in Action

Cpl.	E. ALEXANDER
Tpr.	J.L. BOUCK
	J. HARDING
	S.I. ROBERTSON

Died of Wounds

Tpr.	J. HAWKINS

Died on Service

Tpr.	F.C. STRECKER
	M.G. WALSH

2nd ROYSTONS HORSE
With Clasp 1906
Roll No. 38

Capt.	SYMONS F.H.
Lt.	GAYLARD E.R.
	TAYLOR S.
	WEBSTER A.E.A.
S/M	COOPER S.
QMS	PALMER F.C.P.
Sgt.	GOLDSWAIN A.E.
	MATHER R.D.
	SHORT H.
	TROW H.A.
Sgt.	WILLIAMSON D.
	WRIGHT E.C.
Cpl.	BENTLEY F.M.
	DALY V.H.
	DEAN A.G.
	ELSE R.J.
	FARRELL J.J.
	HUNTER P.J.
	PARRISH W.H.
	PATTLE F.M.O.
	WAINWRIGHT G.A.
	WEBB O.R.
	WILLMER H.R.
Tmptr.	JONES E.
Pte.	ALTENKIRCH F.J.
	BARBOUR G.R.
	BEATTIE C.W.
	BEATTIE F.S.
	BLANCK E.A.
	BROOKS C.R.
	BUTCHER H.
	CLARKE W.
	CREBO W.R.S.
	CUTHBERT G.
	DANIELS G.
	DE REUCK D.W.
	DE REUCK S.J.
	DU PLESSIS A.
	GALLEYMORE G.
	GAYLARD A.W.
	GLEESON E.A.
	GODFREY M.E.
	GOODALL E.A.
	HALL C.G.
	HALL S.L.
	HAVILAND J.D.
	HAYNES P.O.
	HEMMING G.K. de V.
	HIBBINS W.T.
	HOWE H.C.
	HUMPHREY W.H.
	JONES G.
	KENNEDY L.T.
	KIRK C.B.
	KNAGG H.
	KREUSCH W.C.
	KROPF A.F.
	LONGBOTTOM E.H.
	MacKAY A.
	MacKENZIE J.
	McDONALD S.D.
	McGILL M.
	McKENZIE J.
	MEADE C.R.
	MILES J.Y.
	MINETT W.R.
	NORBYE C.J.
	OHLSON C.
	OHLSON G.A.
	PALMER H.E.
	PATTLE C. St.J.
	PATTLE H.A.
	PAUTZ R.
	RADUE W.C.
	REWITZKY E.J.
	REX C.E.H.
	RICHARDSON R.L.
	ROOS C.J.
	SADI F.
	SAUNDERS W.E.P.
	SCHONKNECHT J.A.H.

Pte.   SHORE W.
        SIMPSON O.
        SWART A.J.
        SWART F.J.
        THOMAS A.W.
        TROW E.J.
        WAKEFORD S.D.
        WALKER T.
        WELSH R.
        WHITMILL E.
        WILLIAM H.G.
        WILLIAMS R.J.

Total of 93 Awards

With Clasps - 93

No Clasps - Nil

Died on Service

Pte.   C. OHLSON

SEARCHLIGHT SECTION
With Clasps 1906
Roll No. 22

Capt.   RITCHIE A. Mc.G.
Gnr.   BOYLE J.   (N.F.A.)
        DRAPER   (N.F.A.)

Total of 3 Awards

With Clasps - 3

No Clasps   - Nil

SIBINDIES LEVIES
With Clasp 1906
Roll No. 27

Sub.Ldr.   JOHNSON S.

Total of 1 Award with Clasp

SUNDRY RECIPIENTS
With Clasp 1906
Rolls 53 & 56

Col.   WOOLLS-SAMPSON Sir A.   KCB
Lt.Col.   ADDISON F.
           Comdt. Stanger
           BOUSFIELD H.R.
           Supernumerary Staff
           FOXON F.E.
           Comdt. Ixopo
           McCUBBIN T.
           Comdt. Durban
           MOLYNEUX W.H.A.
           Natal Militia Staff
           NOBLE R.
           Supernumerary Staff
           SANGMEISTER F.A.W.
           Comdt. Port Shepstone
Major   CROOKSHANK C.
           MAXWELL T.
           Comdt. Dundee
           MENNE T.
           Comdt. Greytown

Capt.   BRU-de-WOLD T.W.
           Mapping Detachment
Lt.   BEACHCROFT R.H.
           Comdt. Vryheid Dist.
           MARITZ A.J.S.
           Comdt. Melmoth Dist.
           MATTHEWS M.
           Comdt. Dundee
           WHEELWRIGHT W.G.
           Asst. Comdt. Verulam
Maj.Gen.   STEPHENSON F.E.   No Clasp
Lt.Col.   GREENWOOD H.S.   No Clasp
           C.S.A.R.C.
Major   HAYES-SADLER R.   No Clasp
           Special Service
Lt.   FITZGERALD E.   No Clasp
           Field Intelligence

Total of 20 Awards

With Clasps - 16

No Clasps   - 4

TRANSVAAL MEDICAL STAFF CORPS.
With Clasp 1906
Roll No. 25

Capt.   POSNETT W.G.
Sgt.   DEXTER W.H.
Pte.   CROCKHART J.H.
        DEFRIES W.
        JEAFFRESON A.C.
        McGONIGAL J.E.
        MILLIGAN W.A.
        MORRIS S.
        NORTON J.H.

Total of 9 Awards - With Clasps

TRANSVAAL MOUNTED RIFLES
With Clasp 1906
Roll No. 36

Lt.Col.   BARKER W.F.   DSO
Major   PERN N.
            PICKBURN W.H.
Capt.QM   PEET G.
Capt.Vet.   HOLLINGHAM E.A.
Capt.   DOBSON R.T.
            JARDINE W.   DSO
            LIGHTERWOOD C.E.
            MACKAY H.
            MITCHELL J.T.
            PANCHAUD H.G.L.
Lt.   BETTINGTON A.V.
            FORBES R.G.
            HALL W.B.
            HEAVINGHAM E.
            LIDDLE H.S.
            MARSHALL G.E.W.
            McFARLANE D.C.
            ROSS J.S.
            SANER R.B.
            TRYON S.
2/Lt.   BRUCE W.
            CRAWLEY A. St.C.
            DELANEY P.
            FORBES J.D.
            GEDDES W.L.
            HEWISON G.W.

2/Lt.	HOOD C.W.		Cpl.	SEETON H.E.
	NEVILLE S.L.			STRINGER F.W.
	PHILLIPS F.D.			STURGEON G.N.
	STORER D.D.			SUGDEN J.M.
	THOMPSON J.W.			WILLIAMS G.W.
RSM	GARNHAM G.W.			WOOD E.
RQMS	SAVAGE W.G.			WOODCOCK G.
Farr.QMS	MESSAGE J.H.			WOODS W.
SQMS	CASTLE A.G.			YOUNG W.
	JONES F.P.		L/Cpl.	AINSLIE A.
	STEWART J.			ANDERSON R.
	WARREN E.C.			BUDD F.C.
SSM	DANDRIDGE E.			CAMERON A.C.
	FIELDING A.F.P.			CONNOR A.F.
	SLY A.W.			FERGUSON F.C.
	TIDBOALD A.E.			FINDLAY S.B.
S/Sgt.	CLARKE W.			FRENCH J.
	DEXTER W.H.			GOODE J.
Farr/Sgt.	CARTER J.			HAAGNER A.C.
	LAMB A.			HAINES S.R.
	MITCHELL C.B. DCM			HAMER D.J.
	MOCHAN J.			HARVEY S.F.
Sad.Sgt.	WILSON A.C.			HAYWOOD W.
Sgt.	BAWCETT W.G.			HERBERT R.W.
	BECHINA A.			HOLMES A.S.
	BRAND E.B. MSM			HOLMES R.E.
	DAVIES J.Y.			JOHNSON H.
	DAWSON J.T.			JOHNSTONE G.M.
	DONOHUE T.			KENNEDY F.F.
	GIBBS A.W.			KNIGHT T.
	HOLDER C.H.			LEIGH A.E.T.
	HOLDSWORTH A.			McEVOY P.
	HORWOOD D.			NEWSON J.A.
	JOHNSTONE J.			O'KEEFE P.
	MALAN F.L. MSM			PEBBLES J.W.
	MINCHIN J.H.			POLE J.H.R.
	PARKE R.D.			ROWELL J.
	ROBERTS C.D.			STOKES J.
	SMITH M.N.			TAYLOR C.
	STONCHAM C.			TICE G.P.
	WADDELL R.A.			WAKEFIELD W.P.
	WES T.			WILKINSON W.S.
	WHITE H.			WINCKWORTH L.E.D.
	WOODFORD H.		Tpr.	ABERDEEN C.H.
A/Sgt.	YOUNG J.J.			ABSOLEM J.L.
S/Cpl.	MITCHELL T.M.			ALLENBURG J.
	WHITEFOOT G.			ANDERSON J.M.
	WHITESIDE A.F.			APPLIN F.H.
	WHYTE J.			ARMSTRONG G.
Cpl.	BAKER A.W.			BAKER J.G.
	BELL E.			BALL H.
	BENSON J.			BAMFORD H.M.
	BOLT H.H.			BANKS H.W.
	CHAPPELL J.			BARBOUR H.F.
	CLAYTON E.M.			BARRETT C.C.
	COOKE H.			BARRETT E.
	DUNN H.			BARRIE J.S.
	FERGUSON G.			BELL S.W.
	FRAGLEY C.E.			BENNETT C.G.
	GREENFIELD J.K.			BENNETTS J.
	HARVEY W.			BENTLEY A.F.
	KEWLEY C.			BLACK A.
	LEAL A.			BLAINE B.L.
	LURCOCK R.M.			BLANKLEY G.
	MacLEAN J.K.			BLUNDEN B.V.
	MARLOWE J.E.			BLYTHER L.C.
	MOORE J.H.			BODLEY G.H.
	NAUCARROW S.H.			BOOTH J.B.
	OTT H.			BOWDEN E.
	ROGERS G.P.			BOWMAN G.
	ROSS A.S.			BOYTON A.E.
	RUDDOCK J.W.			BRADLEY F.H. VC

Tpr.	BRANSGROVE H.E.	Tpr.	FORDHAM S.A.
	BRIGHT G.J.		FRAME D.
	BRODRICK L.A.		FRAME W.
	BROOK S.		FRANKLIN C. de M.
	BROOMFIELD A.		FRANKLIN J.G.
	BROSMAN M.P.		FROST T.O.
	BROWN A.		GAMMIE W.L.
	BROWNE G.		GATLAND E.F.
	BUCK S.J.		GEDDES V.J.
	BUCKRIDGE N.F.D.		GEORGE F.R.
	BUNDOCK E.J.		GEORGE W.
	BUTLER H.E.		GIBSON W.S.
	BYRNS W.J.		GIDDEY C.L.
	CALDICOTT H.S.		GILBERT A.
	CAMERON D.		GIMOUR T.
	CARD L.O.C.		GLOVER F.H.
	CARLRICK F.		GOODLIFFE J.
	CASEY J.		GOODMAN T.A.
	CAVEN J.		GOODWIN D.J.
	CHANEY J.		GORDON A.
	CHAPMAN J.T.		GORDON J.H.
	CHRIMES W.D.		GRANGER E.W.
	CLARK J.A.		GREENE W.H.
	CLARKE R.C.		GRENFELL J.
	COCKBURN J.		GREY W.
	COCKERTON J.		GRUBB R.R.
	COHN L.J.		HALLEY J.
	COMLEY W.		HARPUR E.
	COOK H.F.		HARPUR W.
	COTTS E.O.		HARRISON W.T.L.
	CREDIE J.		HAWLEY T.
	CREWE R.H.		HAYTON A.C.
	CROSBY F.J.		HEATH A.H.
	CRUESS W.N.		HEELEY W.H.
	CULSHAW J.J.		HEINEKEY G.P.
	CUMMING C.L.		HERLIHY G.P.
	CUMMING D.W.		HIGGINSON H.
	CUMMINS J.		HIGGINSON T.
	DANIELS J.C.		HIGSON F.W.
	DANSEY H.W.G.		HILL W.N.
	DAVIDSON A.		HODGKINS S.
	DAVIES J.W.		HONAN E.
	DAVIS D.J.		HOPKINS C.
	DAY T.L.		HORGAN P.
	DEAN H.		HOSFORD F.
	DE SALAS J.P.C.		HOSKYN C.H.
	DE WITT A.B.		HOWARD G.S.
	DIXON W.M.		HOWE W.
	DOUGLAS J.		HOY A.E.
	DOUGLAS J.W.		HUDSON W.G.
	DOUGLAS W.J.		HUNT C.T.
	DRAPPER J.R.		ISINMONGER R.B.
	DRYSDALE L.		IVES S.A.
	DUNLOP J.G.		JACKSON C.
	ECKOUT P.J.L.		JAMES D.H.
	EGERTON T.J.		JAMES J.H.
	EISEN C.A.		JANE W.A.
	ELLABY F.N.		JEFFREY G.R.
	EMMS F.		JEFFREY H.M.
	ERICSEN G.		JEFFREYS C.A.
	ESKRITT A.J.		JOBSON R.H.
	EVANS J.M.		JOHN S.C.
	FALCONER W.G.		JOHNSTON E.A.
	FELL A.S.		JOHNSTONE A.S.
	FIFEFIELD G.O.		JONES C.
	FILLERERY J.G.		JONES J.
	FINLAYSON R.J.		JOUBERT A.F.
	FLEURY A.		KEITH A.
	FLOWER J.		KESSELL W.H.
	FLOYD G.J.		KINGDON A.F.
	FORDHAM E.E.		KLINE M.F.

Tpr.	KNIGHT R.B.	Tpr.	PRICE T.
	LANGER E.F.J.		PRIME H.J.
	LESLIE W.		PULLEN J.C.
	LEWIS O.T.		PURCHASE O.S.
	LIDDLOW C.C.		RAINES H.
	LILLICO R.		REDMOND C.F.
	LISSACK H.		REECE P.M.
	LORRAINE J.B.		REID F.V.W.
	LOWERY H.		REID J.H.
	LUMLEY A.		REIDIE T.
	MacGREGOR D.		RICHARDSON A.T.
	McGREGOR D.S.		RICHMOND G.F.
	MALCOLMSON T.		RICHTER A.P.
	MALPAGE V.		RIPPER G.W.
	MANSON J.S.		ROBERTSON A.H.
	MARE S.D.		ROBINSON H.
	AMRRIOTT T.		ROCHE M.F.
	MARSHALL W.F.		RODDA S.
	MARSHALL W.L.		RODIE J.W.
	MARTIN H.R.		ROGERS A.W.
	MATHER J.		ROSEVEARE W.
	MAWBY W.H.		RUSH T.W.
	McBRIDE A.		RYAN J.L.
	McDONALD J.A.		SAUNDERSON J.
	McGREGOR A.D.		SAWYER R.E.
	McGREGOR C.		SCOTT G.P.
	McILVENNA C.J.		SCOTT J. (1044)
	McKAY A.		SCRIMGEOUR J.
	McKENZIE A.E.		SCRIMGEOUR P.
	McKRELL H.E.		SHALDERS H.
	McLEAN R.		SHARPE D.S.
	McLEOD D.		SHEANEN T.C.
	McLEISH D.		SHEARD H.C.
	McMILLAN W.		SHIPWAY R.J.
	McNEIL C.G.		SIMCOX F.
	MILTON J.M.		SIMPSON F.L.
	MITCHELL S.G.		SIVEWRIGHT W.D.
	MOOLMAN H.		SKILL N.J.
	MORGAN W.		SMITH E.
	MORRIS W.J.		SMITH G.B.
	MORRISON A.		SMITH G.S.
	MYBURG P.		SMITH H.W.
	NAPPER E.R.		SMITH R.B.
	NEILSON T.		SMITH R.M.
	NEWMAN W.		SMITHSON H.A.
	NICHOLSON J.		STERICKER W.
	OGDEN T.H.		STEYN H.W.
	O'HEA P.W.		STEYTLER G.B.
	OLDS A.A.		STORM A.
	ORBELL A.		STRANACK W.
	ORBELL J.		STRANG J.
	O'REILLY J.E.		STUART A.W.
	OXENHAM H.A.		SUFFERN J.
	PAATZ O.M.		SULLIVAN P.
	PALM R.G.B.		SUTHERLAND J.H.
	PARKER H.E.		SWAN R.J.
	PARKS F.		SYMINGTON Q.L.A.
	PARRY J.E.		TAINTON F.B.
	PARSON W.		TATCHELL J.
	PARSONSON E.C.		TAYLFORTH T.
	PATRICK A.		THOMALLA A.W.
	PATTINSON W.		THOMAS T.M.
	PEACOCK C.W.		THOMPSON C.
	PEMBERTHY J.		THOMPSON J.B.
	PENNY E.		THORNE T.L.
	PHILLIPS H.E.		THUNDER E.Q.
	PIGGEN F.		TICE C.H.
	PIKE O.		TOBIN W.
	PILKINGTON K.J.		TOWNSEND R.W.
	PLASKETT J.W.		TREMEEN T.H.
	PLINT H.O.		UYS J.H.C.
	POLLARD G.		VAN BEEK T.H.

Tpr. VAUGHAN L.
      VENABLES F.W.
      VENN C.H.B.
      VISSER G.S.
      WAGNER J.
      WALKER J.
      WALKER T.M.
      WARD R.
      WARDLEY T.C.
      WEBBER J.W.
      WEBSTER T.
      WEIL L.G.
      WELLS F.
      WESTOLL A.
      WHALLEY J.
      WHARRAM M.
      WHEELER J.F.
      WHITE E.M.
      WHITE J.W.
      WILLIAMS G.H.
      WILLOWS T.O.
      WINDER J.
      WISEMAN J.H.D.
      WOODCOCK G.
      WOODS W.T.
      WOODWARD W.E.
      WRIGHT A.H.
      WYNNE M.W.
      YOUNG H.
      YOUNG W.N.
      ZAHARIA J.

Without Clasps

Capt.   ASHFIELD W.W.
           CURREY E.F.N.
           MacFARLANE S.C.   DSO
Chaplain   HILL E.
Lt.   MARTIN R.S.
           RAPP C.S.
Condr.   ARLE C.
           CHRISTIAN R.E.
           ISAAC F.W.
Tpr.   ALCOCK T.O.
           ANDOW S.E.
           ATHERTON J.H.
           BLUETT R.T.
           BOTHA F.J.
           BURGE T.
           CASTLE H.
           COCKSEDGE B.
           CURRIE J.O.
           DES FOUNTAIN F.A.
           DOUGLAS J.W.
           DU PLESSIS F.O.
           DU PLESSIS P.J.
           FISHER A.C.
           FLANNIGAN W.
           FULTON J.B.
           GOODWIN W.H.
           HERSON S.F.
           JOHNSON W.S.
           JURGENSON T.E.
           KELSALL V.A.
           KING C.D.
           KITTER C.M.
           LONG C.H.L.
           MAW H.C.
           McCLINTOCK C.
           McDOWELL T.
           SCOTT J. (839)
           SCRIMGEOUR W.H.
           SEDGWICK J.K.

Tpr.   SHERET W.
           SHORT E.
           SMALLBERGER A.
           STUART J.
           WALDEN H.E.
           WILLIAMS E.
           YORKE A.F.R.

Total of 535 Awards

With Clasps - 489

No Clasps - 46

Note: Tpr. F.H. Bradley V.C. - The Award of the Victoria Cross was for an action on 26th September 1901 at ITA (Zululand) whilst he was a Driver with the 69th Battery - R.F.A.

Killed in Action

Tpr.   R.B. Knight on 2.7.1906
Capt. S.C. MacFarlane DSO on 10.6.1906

Died of Wounds

Tpr.   F.H. Glover - Wounded on 13.6.06
       H.C. MAW - Wounded on 14.5.06
       H.W. Steyn - on 20.6.1906

The Following Civilians with the **TRANSVAAL MOUNTED RIFLES,** had their names submitted for the medal and clasp. NO AWARDS WERE MADE.

THOMAS MILLER   : War Correspondent
                  Rand Daily Mail.
W.J. POWELL   : War Correspondent
                  Transvaal Leader.
T. BRITTIAN   : Photographer
                  Transvaal Leader.

TRANSVAAL VOLUNTEER STAFF
With Clasps 1906
Roll No. 31

Bt.Col.   BRIGGS C.J.
Bt.Maj.   LAMONT J.W.F.
Major   ROWLAND M.C.

Total of 3 Awards - With Clasps

TRANSVAAL VOLUNTEER TRANSPORT CORPS.
With Clasp 1906
Roll No. 31

Major   KING C.E.S.

Total of 1 Award - With Clasp

UMSINGA MILITIA RESERVES
With Clasp 1906
Roll No. 54

Chief
Leader   MULLER A.
           STRYDOM T.J.
Sub.Ledr. WALKER C.E.

Sgt.	CALDWELL R.A.		Cpl.	NEL D.A.
Tpr.	BROEKMAN C.H.			NEL J.A.
	WHELAN V.L.			REDINGER E.
				VAN ROOYEN I.L.
				VAN ROOYEN W.

No Clasps Issued

Leader	DE JAGER F.J.		Tpr.	ANGUS G.A.D.
	STRYDOM P.D.			BEANLAND F.
	STRYDOM W.W.			BOTHA G.M.
Sub.Ledr.	SAUNDERS G.S.			BRAITHWAITE P.H.
QMS	CLACKLAN I.G.			CADLE J.F.
Sgt.	STRYDOM F.R.			DEGENAAR P.H.
	WOHLBERG W.H.			DITTRICH F.A.
Cpl.	DEDEKIND H.W.			EKSTEEN C.
	DU BOIS C.			ERFMAN F.
	KOCHER P.			GUNTER D.
	SCHRAAM A.			HARDMAN W.H.
	SHEPHERD G.R.			HAVEMAN C.E.
Tpr.	ADAMS C.			HAVEMEN J.D.
	ADAMS H.			HAVEMAN J.S.
	ADAMS W.			HAVEMAN O.H.
	BAKEBERG W.			KASSIER B.
	BOND H.R.P.			KRUGER J.J.
	CHANDLEY A.			LILJE H.W.
	COMBRING I.H.			MARE D.J.
	COMBRING I.S.			MARE P.
	DANIEL B.S.			MARITZ J.
	DEDEKIND J.			MARTENS C.J.
	DEDEKIND T.H.			McGEE J.G.
	FINNING H.F.			McKENZIE W.S.
	GIBB G.D.C.			NEL C.J.
	KLENGUNBERG A.			NEL J.C.
	KORHS C.			NEL J.J.
	LEISAGANG I.			NEL J.J.
	MARKHAM W.			NEL L.J.
	MICHALEY N.			NEL L.L.
	MULLER E.			NEL P.
	OOSTHUESEON I.			NORTON G.H.
	STRYDOM G.			PERRY M.J.
	STRYDOM H.J.			PORTER J.H.
	STRYDOM I.I.			RALL J.
	STRYDOM J.J. Snr.			REDINGER G.
	STRYDOM S.L.			SCHAFER F.C.
	VOLKER T.			SWARTZ N.J.
	WILSON J.			VANDER BERG A.P.
	WOHLBERG W.H. Jnr.			VAN HELSDINGEN G.
				VAN ROOYEN A.C.J.
				VAN ROOYEN G.I.

Total of 46 Awards

With Clasps - 6

No Clasps - 40

				VAN ROOYEN L.J.
				VAN ROOYEN T.C.
				VAN ZUYDAM I.J.

UMVOTI DIVISION RESERVES
With Clasp 1906
Roll No. 46

No Clasps Issued

Chief			Q/M	HANDLEY G.
Leader	NEL J.A.		QMS	HIBBERT W.
Leader	LANDSBERG R.		Cpl.	BOTHA J.J.
Adj.	BOTHA R.P.			LILJE K.H.
Sub.				SWARTZ J.J.
Leader	NEL A.I.J.		Tpr.	GUNTER H.
	VERMAAK C.J.			HARRISON T.
O.R.Sgt.	EDWARDS J.S.			HAVEMAN F.R.
Sgt.	KUNZ J.J.			HAVEMEN J.
	NEL J.H.R.			HAVEMAN S.C.
	VAN ROOYEN P.H.			HAVEMAN V.A.
Cpl.	MARITZ L.			HILL L.
	MARTENS J.J.			HUBER A.L.
				KORSTEN J.S.
				MARE J.T.
				NEL C.J.
				NEL O.G.
				POST G.

Tpr.	ROLFE E.H.		Sgt.	LAURENCE A.
	ROTTCHER K.P.F.			LYLE H.A.P.
	ROTTCHER M.C.			McCREADIE H.
	SCHAFER H.F.			McGEE J.
	STADLER E.			NISH W.
	STEEL H.S.			NYBERG A.
	STEVENS J.			OELLERMANN H.R.F.
	TATHAM C.			RIXON R.J.
	WARWICK C.C.			RUDLING W.G.

Total of 88 Awards

With Clasps - 61

No Clasps - 27

Killed in Action
Tpr.   H.S. STEEL

UMVOTI MOUNTED RIFLES
With Clasp 1906
Roll No. 26

Col.	LEUCHARS G. CMG DSO	Sgt. (cont.)	SHORT J.W.
Major	CARTER S.		SMITH C.J.
	NEWMARCH W.J.S.		TORLAGE H.F.
	PLANT H.G.		TORLAGE J.R.
Capt.	ANGUS W.N.		WERNER P.
	GALLWEY W.J.	Cpl.Sad.	SMITH F.S.
	LANDSBERG M.		SUTTON H.
	REICHE J.C.	Cpl.SS.	HORMANN H.F.W.
	SIMKINS E.		LAWRENCE P.J.
Lt.	ARMITAGE J.W.	Cpl.	BOND H.C.
	BROWNING W.J.		CADLE H.A.R.
	FANNIN H.E.G.		CRAIK J.F.
	FITZGERALD M.		CRONJE P.C.
	HARKNESS J.H.		ELLIOTT J.H.
	MAYNE H.		ELLIOTT J.J.
	NORTON M.		ERFMANN J.
	NUSS J.H.		FANNIN M.G.
	OTTO P.A.R.		FREESE D.
	SANGMEISTER H.		HELLBERG C.
	SCHROEDER H.F.		HOHLS W.
	STANDFORD H.S.		HOOPER H.
	TURNER E.R.		KITCHEN F.F.
Lt/QM	WEARER A.C.		MASON A.A.
RSM	FERGUSON R. DCM		MAYNE H.
QMS	PURCELL H.		McCLYMONT J.S.
SSM	COLLING J.Z.		McDONALD J.W.
	GAYER A.E.		McKENZIE A.J.
	LAATZ J.		OELLERMANN R.
	RAYMOND W.D.		PATTERSON R.
	SMITH S.H.		PICKUP J.
SQMS	FRASER J.D.		PURCHELL A.C.
	HOHLS E.F.H.		SCHROENN W.H.
	LAUE H.		SHORT P.H.
ORS	CARTER F.		STEWART C.A.
Sgt.Farr.	LEPPARD W.		TAYLOR F.R.
Sgt.Tailor			TORLAGE W.H.H.
	KELLY T.		TURPIN G.W.C.
Sgt.Tmptr.	CROSS G.		VAN TONDER C.J.
Sgt.	ADENDORFF C.K.		WEBSTER R.
	ANDERSON J.P.		WESTBROOK W.A.
	DEDEKIND G.H.	Tmptr.	DEDEKIND E.A.W.
	DRUMMOND P.		HUNTLEY C.M.
	EGNER R.		LAWRENCE F.H.
	LAATZ C.		TISSIMAN R.R.
	LANDSBERG W.		WESTBROOK W.H.
	LARKAN J.A.	Tpr.	ADAMS A.
	LAUE W.		ADENDROFF H.J.C.
			AHRENS C.C.H.
			ALLANSON F.J.
			ANDREWS J.A.
			ANGUS F.B.
			ATKINSON W.
			AUBET F.
			AULD J.
			BALMAK E.A.
			BARR T.
			BARRON W.T.
			BATES C.C.
			BAYLEY G.W.
			BAHN G.H.
			BELL D.
			BELL T.R.

Tpr.	BIRD W.F.	Tpr.	HOOPER O.
	BLOEMEYER W.J.		HOOPER W.
	BOTHA G.P.		HOOPER W.G.
	BRAITHWAITE C.V.		ISSEL C.G.
	BRAITHWAITE E.H.		JAEGER F.O.
	BRAITHWAITE J.W.		KELLY J.J.
	BRAND J.B.		KEMP G.F.
	BROWNING J.		KNOWLES H.
	BUCKLEY H.M.		KOHLER O.
	BUKES H.		KOHRS O.
	BURE C.		LABUSCHAGNE J.C.L.
	BURE F.		LABUSCHAGNE K.J.
	BURE G.		LABUSCHAGNE P.H.
	CAIN T.		LAKE A.H.
	CAMPBELL A.H.		LAMBIE H.
	CARR R.J.		LANDSBERG A.J.
	CHISHOLM A.		LANDSBERG P.
	CLARK A.		LANG A.
	CLEMENTS S.T.		LARSON T.J.
	CONSTANTINE C.		LAUE O.
	COUNIHAN C.		LeROUX J.H.
	COUNIHAN J.		L'ESTRANGE G.
	COUNIHAN W.		LIGHT H.E.
	CRAIG R.M.		LINDHORST E.
	CRIBBINS J.		LUXFORD I.
	CROUCH A.E.		MacPHERSON J.
	CUBITT R.W.		MANTON G.
	DANIEL A.V.		MARE C.J.
	DAWSON F.		MARE F.R.
	DEDEKIND H.C.W.		MARE J.A.
	DEKKER D.J.		MARE L.J.
	DEKKER J.J.		MARE L.J.N.
	DEKKER J.P.C.		MARSHALL E.G.
	DEKKER M.		MARTENS C.C.
	DEKKER N.M.J.		MARTIN R.
	DeWAAL C.S.		MATTHEWS G.
	DeWAAL J.A.		McCHESNEY J.
	DeWALL W.		McKEOWN L.D.M.
	DITTRICH F.W.		McSWENEY P.
	DITTRICH H.W.		MEEK S.
	EDMONDS W.H.H.		MEYER F.
	ERFMANN H.		MINAAR P.
	FANNIN V.G.		NEL J.P.C.
	FINNIE W.		NEL L.J.
	FITZWILLIAM J.		NEL M.G.
	FORRESTER R.M.		NOEL S.
	FRANZ W.		NUSS W.F.
	FREEMAN J.		ODENDAAL W.A.
	FREESE H.		OELLERMANN A.
	FROUDE A.J.		OELLERMANN C.
	GARDEN A.		OELLERMANN J.
	GREEN S.		OELLERMANN T.
	GREEN W.		OLIVIER H.
	GRIFFIN W.		OSBORNE E.E.
	GROVE J.S.		PALEY W.
	HAIGH J.		PARSONS H.A.
	HANSMEYER J.I.		PAVERD H.W.
	HATTINGH C.F.		PENNEY G.
	HATTINGH J.G.		PERFECT G.J.
	HATTINGH J.H.		PFOTENHAUER K.
	HATTINGH J.M.		PHEASANT A.J.
	HATTINGH P.W.J.H.		PHEASANT G.P.W.
	HATTINGH T.J.		PHEASANT G.W.
	HAVEMANN B.		PHEASANT W.F.
	HEINE C.J.		PHELPHS S.
	HEINE E.W.		POPE J.H.
	HENRIKSON E.J.		POST A.
	HILLBRICK W.H.		POST H.
	HIRST C.L.		POST T.
	HODGSON H.A.		POVALL W.F.
	HOHLS C.		RAINER H.
	HOHLS C.F.		RAINER W.

Tpr.	RANDELHOFF C.E.	Sgt.Farr.	JOHNSON J.H.
	RIDLER A.T.	Sgt.	CRAIK C.
	ROBERTS W.P.		HARRIS E.J.
	RODELL A.		JAMES H.A.
	ROLFE R.W.		McKENZIE S.K.G.
	ROSS R.D.		McMICHAEL R.F.
	ROSSMAN H.		SCHROEDER C.
	RUSH J.L.		SCHROEDER G.
	SANSON A.J.		SINCLAIR J.J.
	SARSON J.		TOWNSHEND W.
	SAUNDERS H.	Cpl.	CASTLEDINE L.
	SCHAFER A.W.		DORRINGTON A.E.
	SCHAFER W.K.		EADIE W.
	SCHAFER T.E.		HARRINGTON A.
	SCHALLENBERG H.W.F.		RADCLIFFE D.
	SCHALLENBERG W.J.H.		TISSIMAN J.J.
	SCHOFIELD E.	Tmptr.	KEITH J.A.
	SCHOFIELD G.	Tpr.	ALBERT F.
	SCHRODER E.		ATKINSON S.
	SCOTT J.		BARNES V.E.
	SCRUBBY C.W.		BAXTER F.W.
	SERJEANT T.		BIOLETTE H.O.
	SHARP A.H.		BOAS I.J.
	SHARP C.		BOLLAND E.
	SMIT J.E.		BOWIE D.
	SOWERBY D.		BRIDSON W.
	SPRINGETT E.H.		CAMPBELL J.
	STADLER C.J.		CANT S.G.
	STEGEN H.		CHENEY R.
	STEGEN H.T.O.		COMBRING J.H.
	STEPHENS J.		CORFE R.G.
	STEWART D.		COSGROVE J.
	STEWART W.C.G.		CRADDOCK C.
	STIEGER D.J.		DUCKHAM E.
	STONE J.		ECOB M.
	STRYDOM C.J.		EVANS R.O.
	STRYDOM H.J. (356)		FIELD C.
	STRYDOM H.J. (363)		FITZGERALD M.V.
	STRYDOM H.J. (431)		FLEMING J.A.
	STRYDOM J.H.		GARDNER C.
	TAYLOR V.W.		GILBERT G.
	THOLE A.		GUNN G.
	THOLE E.		HARGREAVES J.
	THOMAS A.E.		HATTENDORFF W.
	TISSIMANN W.E.		HAVEMANN L.J.
	TODD G.T.		HENDERSON S.S.
	TORLAGE R.M.		HEPBURN B.H.
	TORLAGE W.H.		HERON A.E.
	TURNER E.J.		HICKENBOTHAM R.V.
	VAN-den-HEVEN A.J.		HOGG
	VAN-der-LINDEN J.J.		HOPKINS W.G.
	VAN DYK J.J.		HUMPHREY S.
	VAN ROOYEN C.J.		HUNTLEY A.D.
	VAN ROOYEN I.M.		HUTCHINSON W.H.
	VAN ROOYEN J.F.		IZZARD J.
	VARTY E.G.		JAMIESON W.W.
	VARTY R.D.		JONES W.H.
	WASSINK G.C.H.		JOYCE G.T.
	WASSINK W.		KENNEDY A.
	WETENHALL C.W.		KOK I.M.
	WHITE E.S.		KRUGER H.
	WHITE W.G.		LAAS F.C.
	WHITTAKER C.H.		LACKFORD G.W.
	WINTERBOER D.A.		LANDSBERG S.P.
	YOUNG G.		LAPPAN G.N.
	ZIETSMAN I.M.		LONEY T.
			MacMILLAN D.
No Clasps Issued			MARE L.
			MARSHALL F.
Lt/QM	BROWN T.		MARTIN W.
QMS	BLAKE R.L.		McGILLIVRAY D.
ORS	TRILL R.		O'MARA W.H.

Tpr.	PANCHEON T.W.
	POPE W.
	REDINGTON J.H.
	RHIND H.
	RICKARD G.
	RODELL W.
	SCHEEPERS M.J.
	SCHULTZ A.W.
	SELLING H.
	SMITH A.C.
	SMYTHE F.C.
	SOMERS W.R.
	SPARKS F.G.
	SPECKHEIN H.
	THOMAS W.
	THOMAS W.R.
	TORLAGE H.A.
	UGLAND A.D.
	VAN ROOYEN T.J.J.
	VAN TONDER A.J.
	WALKER A.E.D.
	WILSON J.
	WOOD W.L.

Total of 425 Awards

With Clasps - 327

No Clasps - 98

Note: Tpr. H.W.F. Schallenberg had the Clasp issued to him loose on a parade of the NEW HANOVER RESERVE - the duplicate medal was not issued.

ZULULAND CHIEFS
No Clasps Issued
Supplementary Roll

Nkandhla Chiefs
  FULATELAICALA
  HASHI
  LUKULWENI
  MAKUBALO
  MLOTGOTWA
  MNYAKANYA
  SILSHILSHILI
  SIZWANA
  UTSHINANE
  UZINYONGO

Total of 10 Awards

All without Clasps

Nqutu Chiefs
  MAYTIME KA MBUNDA
  GADALENI KA MPIKELELI

Total of 2 Awards

Both without Clasps

Eshowe Chiefs
  MGANDENI
  plus 2 others names not known

Total of 3 Awards

All without Clasps

ZULULAND FIELD FORCE STAFF
With Clasp 1906
Supplementary Roll

Capt.   MULLINS C.H.

Total of 1 Award - with Clasp

ZULULAND MOUNTED RIFLES
With Clasp 1906
Roll No. 5

Major	VANDERPLANK W.A.	
Cap/Adj.	HULLEY D.J.C.	
Capt.	FLINDT R.L.	
Lt/QM	ADAMS C.F.	
Lt.	HEDGES J.S.	
	JAMES H.T.	
	WALTON E.B.	
2nd Lt.	CHAPMAN T.E.	
	COOPER J.R.	
RSM	SMITH L.	
QMS	MOORE T.H.C.	
SSM	CALVERLEY W.J.	DCM
	KING R.F.	
FQMS	PERCIVAL H.	
SQMS	ASHBY J.	
	SHEDLOCK A.B.	
ORS	CLAYTON J.A.W.	
Sgt.	BERRY A.	
	HAZELHURST E.	
	HULLEY A.H.B.	
	OLIVER C.R.	
	TITLESTAD E.	DCM
	WALLACE H.B.	
L/Sgt.	OGDEN J.W.	
Cpl.SS	DORE W.P.	
Cpl.	GUNDERSEN G.M.	
	HANCOCK R.W.	
	McALISTER R.H.	
	PARR C.E.	
	WEBER H.	
L/Cpl.	DU PREEZ J.G.	
	OWEN H.	
Tmptr.	TALLANTIRE H.H.	
Tpr.	ACKERMAN J.	
	ALLEN A.E.	
	ASHBURY H.J.	
	BARNARD M.G.	
	BLANCHE J.F.	
	BOND W.H.	
	BORGEN M.F.	
	BOTHA C.G.	
	BEZUIDENHUIT G.P.J.	
	BEZUIDENHUIT L.M.	
	CHANDLER H.B.	
	CHANDLER R.W.	
	CHAPLIN H.	
	CLARKE A.J.	
	CLARKE H.	
	COLL G.	
	COPE G.E.	
	CORNELIUS J.J.	
	CORNELIUS W.C.J.	
	DEELEY W.	DCM
	DELANEY M.	
	DOMVILLE C.H.	
	DUFF C.H.	
	DUNCAN C.E.	
	DUNCAN C.H.	
	ELS C.J.	

Tpr.	ELS J.C.H.
	FAYE I.
	FERREIRA S.P.
	FOSTER A. (015)
	FOSTER A. (016)
	GIELINK A.B.
	GIELINK A.G.
	GIELINK J.H.
	GIELINK J.M.
	GIELINK R.J.
	GIELINK W.
	GREEN B.E.J.
	HERBST C.J.C.
	HERBST M.J.H.
	HERBST S.J.
	HORNE R.G.P.
	HULLEY A.H.B.
	HUNTER J.Y.
	HURNING G.J.
	JOHNSON A.R.
	JOHNSON C.W. DCM
	JONES W.E.
	KOEKEMOER T.C.
	KRITZINGER L.J.R.
	KRUGER E.H.C.
	LAW W.
	LE ROUX A.S.
	LIVERSAGE H.A.
	LIVERSAGE H.B.
	LIVERSAGE W.M.
	MANNING E.J.
	MARITZ J.G.
	MARITZ T.C.
	MAXTED W.P.
	McLEOD C.T.
	McLEOD H.E.
	McRAE J.
	MOOLMAN J.P.
	MOORE C.W.
	MOORE R.
	MYKLEGAARD F.
	NORD O.
	NORGAARD O.
	NORGAARD K.
	OLIVIER G.O. DCM
	OOSTHUIZEN P.C.
	POTGEITER F.J.
	PRETORIUS A.L.
	PRETORIUS W.J.
	QUANDT VON EICHHOLTZ F.A.G.
	SCHMIDT C.
	SMITH F.R.
	SMITH M.J.
	SPOTSWOOD J.H.
	STEVENS E.
	TALLANTIRE T.G.
	TITLESTAD N.
	TITLESTAD P.E.
	VAN DEN HEEVER D.J.
	VAN DER PLANK V.H.
	VAN ROOYEN C.L.
	VAN ROOYEN D.J.
	VAN ROOYEN G.F.
	VERMAAK J.S.
	WANG H.

No Clasps Issued

Sgt.	LURRING F.R.L.
	WOOD C.F.
Cpl.	DREYER F.

Tpr.	ALLEN C.B.
	ARBUTHNOT H.G.W.
	BOSMAN J.
	BUCK T.J.
	BURN A.N.
	CARLYLE T.
	DAY A.T.
	DUNCAN A.
	FENNELL R.
	FOY S.T.
	FREEMAN F.A.
	GARDINER F.W.
	GOULD L.A.
	GREGG W.H.
	HARGREAVES R.
	JOHNSON H.L.
	LEWIS A.H.
	MURGITROYD W.
	O'CONNOR J.
	PAXTON J.F.
	PETERS W.
	PRIVETT H.W.
	RAFFERTY J.
	ROBERTSON F.
	RUSSEN A.C.
	SHEPPERSON B.M.
	THOMPSON A.
	WEIR J.B.

Total of 155 Awards

With Clasps - 124

No Clasps - 31

Died of Wounds

Tpr.   G. COLL

ZULULAND NATIVES
No Clasps Issued
Supplementary Roll

Induna   KAFULA
Nkandhla Natives
　　　　　MADAKAVANA
　　　　　MANYOUYANA
　　　　　MAPOYISA
　　　　　MGELE
　　　　　MISO
　　　　　MVUKAZI
　　　　　MZWANGEDWA
　　　　　NDASANA
　　　　　NGCEDE
　　　　　NGUNYANGUNYA
　　　　　NKOTENI
　　　　　NKUNYA
　　　　　NTIKI
　　　　　NTSHINANA
　　　　　SIBIJA ADAM
　　　　　SIVELA
　　　　　UPISEYAKA
　　　　　USIYANA
　　　　　UTENI
　　　　　UTSHUDLWANA
　　　　　ZWELEKULE
Nqutu Natives
　　　　　AMOS MKIZE KA MACIMBI
　　　　　BATALANZI
　　　　　MSWARELO KA MAKAYA

Nqutu Natives
    NDUKUYAKE
    NGUMANA KA NONGILA
    NGWENI KA MLAMULA
    SIMON NCOGIKA DAMBUZA

Eshowe Natives
N.Con. BUKUDA
      GEDE
      MLOMONKA
      NADUMBI

Total of 33 Awards

All Without Clasps

ZULULAND POLICE
With Clasp 1906
Roll No. 48 & Supplementary

S/Major	ZAZENE
Sgt.	FATTY
	JAN
	NAHASHAHASH
	NANKANFANA
	NATUTA
	NBATSHANA
	NCYELA
	NLOMOBOMVU
	ZIMBULELI
Cpl.	DAVID
	GAMBUSHI
	GEORGE
	KOMANA
	NONGGAI
Pte.	ABEL
	BANGINDOWA
	BEDJANA
	BILLY
	BONABANYE
	BONIYAKI
	CAGITI
	DOGOZA
	ENOCH
	FUNJANA
	GALA
	GUNDA
	HLABANTU
	HLABATI
	IMPYIPELA
	IZINYO
	JACOB
	JANTONI
	JAZI
	JIM
	JIMBOYI
	JONAS
	KOHWANA
	KOBANE
	KUKUNGITSHA
	LOZO
	LUKALWENI
	MABONA
	MACALA
	MAFA
	MAGIANE
	MAKATAZA
	MAKONZA
	MAKOQUANA
	MANGA
	MANGAPI
	MANGATSHA
Pte.	MANQABA
	MANSIMINI
	MANZANA
	MASOKA
	MASWCINKOSI
	MATOLENDHLALA
	MAZONDO
	MAZWE
	MBOMBO
	MBOMO
	MBOTSHWA
	MBOYIANA
	MBUSWANA
	MGANTSHELWA
	MGITSHWA
	MGWABA
	MGWAIZA
	MHLANANYELWA
	MHLUTULA
	MLANDU
	MOZO
	MPUMBULUZO
	MQIBA
	MSENTENI
	MSIMBUI
	MTIBELI
	MTSHWAIZA
	MTSHYAPANSI
	MUNGUZULU
	MUNTSWINKINI
	MUNTUWINKOSI
	MVIMBI
	MVUMENI
	NAPELU
	NDABAZONKE
	NDENI
	NDUNASELWA
	MGAMIANA
	NGANGEZWA
	MGUNGUZANA
	NKANTOLO
	NKOMO
	NKOMO II
	NOGWATSHA
	NOKIYELA
	NOZENZE
	NTABENI
	NTEKANE
	NTUMENI
	NYAMANA
	SIFUBAZIYAZI
	SIQOBOZI
	SIQOPO
	SITYITYIBALANA
	SKOTSHMANA
	SOMSAYO
	SOMSEU
	SOPIGAZI
	SPAN
	TOM I
	TOM II
	TSHINEYANA
	UGUQA
	UJAN
	UKABANA
	VEBA
	WEZA
	ZANGA
	ZONDOLENI
	ZONKE

No Clasps Issued

Pte.	BATSHOBANE
	ELI
	GINGINHLOVU
	ISIBAMU
	JEVUSA
	JOHN WILLIAM
	LUSWANI
	LUSWAYE
	MABUNU
	MALI
	MAMANKA
	MANGATI
	MATINYANA
	MATSHEIN
	MDAGELWA
	MIGIDI
	MUNGWANA
	MZINDI
	NDHLENDHLA
	SISINI
	SKONKWANA
	UFAGWEZWE
	UKANYEZA
	UTOLI
	ZUMPANA

Total of 147 Awards

With Clasps - 122

No Clasps   - 25

Note: The handwritten Roll has confusing M's and N's, so it is possible that some of the names listed have been spelt incorrectly.

LOOSE CLASPS

A note on the Supplementary Roll of 5th March 1909 records the issue of 121 loose clasps, (as these had not been previously issued) to those, on this Roll. There is one exception however, Pte. JIMBOYI, whose medal and clasp was issued to him on a Supplementary Roll of 11th November 1909. Apart from JIMBOYI, all the others on this rill, thus have a LOOSE CLASP to the medal.

SUMMARY OF UNITS, MEDALS & CLASPS

UNIT	WITH CLAPS	WITHOUT CLASP	TOTAL AWARDED	PAGE NO.
AMABOMVU LEVY	NIL	32	32	18
AMAFUNZE TRIBE	NIL	20	20	18
BORDER MOUNTED RIFLES	213	38	251	18
CAPE MOUNTED RIFLES	70	NIL	70	20
CHAPLAINS	4	2	6	21
CIVILIAN EMPLOYEES	NIL	135	135	21
DOCTORS	NIL	4	4	22
DUNDEE BOROUGH RESERVES	NIL	35	35	22
DUNDEE DISTRICT RESERVES	NIL	62	62	22
DUNNS SCOUTS	20	NIL	20	23
DURBAN LIGHT INFANTRY	539	93	632	23
DURBAN MILITIA RESERVES	NIL	194	194	28
ESCOURT MILITIA RESERVES	105	13	118	29
GREYTOWN RESERVES 1st	NIL	42	42	30
GREYTOWN RESERVES 2nd	1	NIL	1	30
H.E. THE GOVERNOR - STAFF	2	1	3	30
IMPERIAL OFFICERS	NIL	4	4	30
INDIAN STRETCHER BEARER CORPS.	NIL	20	20	31
INTELLIGENCE SERVICE	17	34	51	31
KLIP RIVER RESERVES	NIL	62	62	31
KRANTZKOP RESERVES	71	4	75	32
LANCASHIRE & YORKSHIRE CONTINGENCY	150	NIL	150	33
LOWER TUGELA RESERVES	NIL	35	35	34
MELMOTH RESERVES	25	32	57	34
MILITIA RESERVES LOWER TUGELA DIVISION	NIL	52	52	34
MILITIA TRANSPORT SERVICE CORPS.	45	28	73	35
NATAL CARBINEERS	878	132	1010	36
NATAL FIELD ARTILLERY - 1st Bdge.Staff	3	2	5	43
NATAL FIELD ARTILLERY - "A" BATTERY	94	21	115	43
NATAL FIELD ARTILLERY - "B" BATTERY	101	5	106	44
NATAL FIELD ARTILLERY - "C" BATTERY	91	10	101	45
NATAL FIELD ARTILLERY - POM POM SECTION	24	NIL	24	45
NATAL GUIDES	4	NIL	4	46
NATAL MEDICAL CORPS.	104	19	123	46

UNIT	WITH CLASPS	WITHOUT CLASP	TOTAL AWARDED	PAGE NO.
NATAL MILITIA STAFF	30	1	31	47
NATAL MOUNTED RIFLES	424	38	462	47
NATAL NATIVE HORSE	335	3	338	51
NATAL NAVAL CORPS.	136	67	203	53
NATAL POLICE SUPPLEMENTARY	NIL	2	2	55
NATAL POLICE	1082	32	1114	55
NATAL POLICE GAOLERS	50	NIL	50	63
NATAL RANGERS	839	68	907	63
NATAL ROYAL REGIMENT	225	33	258	70
NATAL SERVICE CORPS.	111	8	119	71
NATAL TELEGRAPH CORPS.	38	6	44	72
NATAL VETERINARY CORPS.	11	2	13	73
NEWCASTLE DIVISION RESERVES	NIL	88	88	73
NEW HANOVER RESERVES	NIL	75	75	74
NKANDHLA TOWN GUARD	NIL	17	17	74
NORTHERN DISTRICTS MOUNTED RIFLES	233	6	239	75
NURSES – CIVILIAN	NIL	7	7	76
ROYSTONS HORSE	714	31	745	77
ROYSTONS HORSE 2nd	93	NIL	93	82
SEARCHLIGHT SECTION	3	NIL	3	83
SIBINDIES LEVIES	1	NIL	1	83
SUNDRY RECIPIENTS	16	4	20	83
TRANSVAAL MEDICAL STAFF CORPS.	9	NIL	9	83
TRANSVAAL MOUNTED RIFLES	489	46	535	83
TRANSVAAL VOLUNTEER STAFF	3	NIL	3	87
TRANSVAAL VOLUNTEER TRANSPORT CORPS.	1	NIL	1	87
UMSINGA MILITIA RESERVES	6	40	46	87
UMVOTI DIVISION RESERVES	61	27	88	88
UMVOTI MOUNTED RIFLES	327	98	425	89
ZULULAND CHIEFS	NIL	15	15	92
ZULULAND FIELD FORCE	1	NIL	1	92
ZULULAND MOUNTED RIFLES	124	31	155	92
ZULULAND NATIVES	NIL	33	33	93
ZULULAND POLICE	122	25	147	94
TOTAL	8045	1934	9979	

www.ingramcontent.com/pod-product-compliance
Lightning Source LLC
Chambersburg PA
CBHW081544090426
42743CB00014BA/3131